Lecture Notes in Artificial Intelligence   7838

Subseries of Lecture Notes in Computer Science

LNAI Series Editors

Randy Goebel
University of Alberta, Edmonton, Canada
Yuzuru Tanaka
Hokkaido University, Sapporo, Japan
Wolfgang Wahlster
DFKI and Saarland University, Saarbrücken, Germany

LNAI Founding Series Editor

Joerg Siekmann
DFKI and Saarland University, Saarbrücken, Germany

T0171850

Francesca Giardini
Frédéric Amblard (Eds.)

Multi-Agent-Based Simulation XIII

International Workshop, MABS 2012
Valencia, Spain, June 4-8, 2012
Revised Selected Papers

 Springer

Volume Editors

Francesca Giardini
CNR, LABSS-ISTC
00185 Rome, Italy
E-mail: francesca.giardini@istc.cnr.it

Frédéric Amblard
Université Toulouse 1, IRIT
31042 Toulouse, France
E-mail: frederic.amblard@ut-capitole.fr

ISSN 0302-9743   e-ISSN 1611-3349
ISBN 978-3-642-38858-3   e-ISBN 978-3-642-38859-0
DOI 10.1007/978-3-642-38859-0
Springer Heidelberg Dordrecht London New York

Library of Congress Control Number: 2013939783

CR Subject Classification (1998): I.2.11, I.2, I.6, F.1

LNCS Sublibrary: SL 7 – Artificial Intelligence

Typesetting: Camera-ready by author, data conversion by Scientific Publishing Services, Chennai, India

Printed on acid-free paper

Springer is part of Springer Science+Business Media (www.springer.com)

Preface

The 2012 edition of the Multi-Agent-Based Simulation (MABS) Workshop was the 13th occurrence of a series that began in 1998. The MABS workshop series aims to bring together researchers interested in multi-agent systems and researchers coming from the social sciences, and to provide them with the opportunity to discuss theories and applications for developing new approaches to deal with complex social systems. The scientific focus of MABS lies on the confluence of the social sciences and multi-agent systems, with a strong application/empirical vein, and its emphasis is placed on (a) exploratory agent-based simulation as a principled way of undertaking scientific research in the social sciences and (b) using social theories as an inspiration to new frameworks and developments in multi-agent systems. Thanks to this truly inter-disciplinary approach, complex engineering problems related to agent-based systems can be addressed, and the resulting solutions can be applied in areas as diverse as economics, management, organization science and to the social sciences in general.

The excellent quality of this workshop has been recognized since its inception and its proceedings have been regularly published in Springer's *Lecture Notes in Artificial Intelligence* series. More information about the MABS workshop series may be found at the site http://www.pcs.usp.br/~mabs.

MABS 2012 was hosted at the 11th International Conference on Autonomous Agents and Multi-Agent Systems (AAMAS 2012), which was held in Valencia, Spain, during June 4–8, 2012. In this edition, 35 submissions from 15 countries were received, from which we selected 15 for presentation (near 43% acceptance). The papers presented in the workshop were revised, and eventually extended and reviewed again, and 11 papers were selected for this volume.

We are very grateful to the participants who provided a lively atmosphere of debate during the presentation of the papers and during the general discussion about the challenges that the MABS field faces. We are also very grateful to all the members of the Program Committee and the additional reviewers for their hard work. Thanks are also due to Elisabeth Sklar (AAMAS 2012 Workshop Chair), to Wiebe van der Hoek and Lin Padgham (AAMAS 2012 General Co-chairs), to Vincent Conitzer and Michael Winikoff (AAMAS Program Co-chairs), and to Vicente Botti (AAMAS 2012 Local Organizing Committee Chair).

December 2012

Francesca Giardini
Frédéric Amblard

Organization

General and Program Chairs

Francesca Giardini   LABSS, ISTC, National Research Council, Italy

Frédéric Amblard   IRIT, University Toulouse 1 Capitole, France

MABS Steering Committee

Frédéric Amblard	IRIT, University Toulouse 1 Capitole, France
Luis Antunes	University of Lisbon, Portugal
Rosaria Conte	National Research Council, Italy
Paul Davidsson	Malmö University, Sweden
Nigel Gilbert	University of Surrey, UK
Scott Moss	Manchester Metropolitan University, UK
Keith Sawyer	Washington University in St. Louis, USA
Jaime Simão Sichman	University of São Paulo, Brazil
Keiki Takadama	University of Electro-Communications, Japan

Program Committee

Diana Francisca Adamatti	Universidade Federal do Rio Grande, Brazil
Frédéric Amblard	IRIT, University Toulouse 1 Capitole, France
Luis Antunes	University of Lisbon, Portugal
Joao Balsa	University of Lisbon, Portugal
Carole Bernon	IRIT, Université Paul Sabatier, Toulouse, France
Tibor Bosse	Vrije Universiteit Amsterdam, The Netherlands
Antônio Carlos da Rocha Costa	Universidade Federal do Rio Grande, Brazil
Cristiano Castelfranchi	ISTC/CNR, Italy
Shu-Heng Chen	National Chengchi University, Taiwan
Sung-Bae Cho	Yonsei University, Korea
Helder Coelho	University of Lisbon, Portugal
Paul Davidsson	Malmö University, Sweden
Gennaro Di Tosto	Utrecht University, The Netherlands
Bruce Edmonds	Manchester Metropolitan University, UK
Benoit Gaudou	IRIT, University Toulouse 1 Capitole, France
Armando Geller	Group W, USA
Francesca Giardini	LABSS, ISTC, National Research Council, Italy

Nigel Gilbert	University of Surrey, UK
William Griffin	Arizona State University, USA
Laszlo Gulyas	AITIA International Informatics Inc., Hungary
David Hales	The Open University, UK
Matt Hare	University of Zurich, Switzerland
Rainer Hegselmann	University of Bayreuth, Germany
Wander Jager	University of Groningen, The Netherlands
Marco Janssen	Arizona State University, USA
Satoshi Kurihara	Osaka University, Japan
Eunate Mayor	CNRS-IRIT, France
Jean-Pierre Muller	CIRAD, France
Emma Norling	Centre for Policy Modelling, UK
Paulo Novais	University of Minho, Portugal
Juan Pavon Mestrasb	Universidad Complutense Madrid, Spain
Graçaliz Pereira Dimuro	Universidade Federal do Rio Grande, Brazil
Juliette Rouchier	Greqam/CNRS, France
Jordi Sabater-Mir	IIIA, Spain
David Sallach	Argonne National Lab and University of Chicago, USA
Keith Sawyer	Washington University in St. Louis, USA
Jaime Sichman	University of Sao Paulo, Brazil
Carles Sierra	IIIA, Spain
Liz Sonenberg	University of Melbourne, Australia
Karoly Takacs	Corvinus University of Budapest, Hungary
Keiki Takadama	University of Electro-Communications, Japan
Oswaldo Teran	University of Los Andes, Venezuela
Takao Terano	Tokyo Institute of Technology, Japan
Klaus Troitzsch	University of Koblenz-Landau, Germany
H. Van Dyke Parunak	Vectore Research Centre, USA
Harko Verhagen	Stockholm University, Sweden
Daniel Villatoro	IIIA, Spain
Natalie van der Wal	VU University Amsterdam, The Netherlands

Additional Reviewers

Nardine Osman	IIIA, Spain
Luis Gustavo Nardin	University of São Paulo, Brazil
Allan Diego Silva Lima	University of São Paulo, Brazil

Table of Contents

Simulating Social Behaviour Implementing Agents Endowed with Values and Drives

Gennaro Di Tosto and Frank Dignum

Utrecht University
Department of Information and Computing Sciences
The Netherlands
{g.ditosto,f.p.m.dignum}@uu.nl

Abstract. We present a working model of agent's social behaviour based on drives and values. Drives represent internal needs of the agents; values are used to prioritise them. Discussed in the context of a simulation scenario centred around smoking behaviour in public places, the designed system proves itself useful to tackle issues where agents face conflicting decision's choices, or where agent's behaviour has negative side-effects for other agents.

1 Introduction

In recent years a majority of European countries enacted a ban against smoking in public places like coffee-bars and restaurants. The ban targeted Environmental Tobacco Smoke (ETS) and was intended to protect people from the damage of second-hand smoke.

National reports about compliance with this legislation indicate that the effects of the smoking ban are far from being homogeneous. Italy, for example, among the first countries to introduce a law against ETS, provides an example of widespread compliance, achieved immediately after the enactment of the ban. On the other extreme, in the Netherlands, consistent violations have been documented; consequently, prohibitions have been relaxed and exceptions have been created for all venues smaller than 70 square meters who do not have employees other than the owners.

To explain the different fates of the smoking-ban policy across Europe it is necessary to investigate the complex dynamics of drives and motivation that affect the actions people take. The action an agent takes to satisfy one drive may affect the levels of other drives and may elicit a response from nearby agents. Thus we can see an agent's drives as having a constantly-changing balance, and a group of agents as having a complex web of drives. Many factors play a role in this web; assuming the smoking-ban as a case study, we can select factors that pertain to smoking and environment and, using these factors, consider how drives change and are satisfied or not, and how the above affects overall compliance with the law when it is introduced.

The varied justification and formalisation of the law in different countries allows us to consider how different considerations and representations of values

F. Giardini and F. Amblard (Eds.): MABS 2012, LNAI 7838, pp. 1–12, 2013.

might contribute to the explanation of the stronger or weaker acceptance of the norm and the consequent individual compliance. In framing the ban around different values—i.e. Public health, in the case of Italy, vs. better working conditions, in the Netherlands—legislators have created distinct cultural environments in which the norm operates. The values around which they structure the legislation can be seen as implicit motivation.

In other words, with the introduction of an anti-smoking law, different values are at stake in different settings. The relative weight of these values in the setting, both at the level of the individual and within a larger group, can be regarded as a contributing factor, and may explain the lesser degree of acceptance of the law compared to the acceptance in other seemingly similar settings, like cinemas or restaurants. Particularly connected to the coffee-bar setting are certain values regarding the authority that is accepted, like freedom or autonomy. On the level of behaviour, values include health, care for others (with respect to their health), economic interest (in some countries, e.g. The Netherlands, bar keepers claim their clientele dramatically dropped after the new law went into effect), but also, and importantly: joy or pleasure. The actions agents take to satisfy the drives associated with pleasure in our model derive from the particular structure we use to represent agents' values.

2   The Model

We wanted to give an explicit representation to the implicit motivations of the agent, in this case drives and values, and implement them in a computational model to show how these low-level forces can generate higher-level behavioural patterns that can be used to study a different number of social issues. We selected one related to smoking behaviour because of its illustrative features and current relevance in the European context.

2.1   Values

Values are dispositions to choose one state of the world over another. While formally it is possible to reduce values to an order over a set of alternative outcomes [4], the task to include them in the deliberation cycle of a BDI (Beliefs-Desires-Intentions) agent is less straightforward, mainly due to the overlap between the concept of value and other relevant mental constructs, like: beliefs, goals and desires, and norms.

Miceli and Castelfranchi [5] define values as a special kind of evaluation. Such an evaluation 'consists of an assumption of agent E (Evaluator) about X's power (means, properties, capabilities, skills) to reach a certain goal G.' An evaluation informs the agent that the entity X (be it a tool, another agent, an institution, etc.) is a good means to reach a specific end. What happens with values is that the notion of the goal against which we are evaluating X disappears, hence X becomes "good" in itself, and the agent holding the value pursues it through terminal goals, instead of as a means for something else.

In this perspective values are implicit evaluations: they are still susceptible of practical reasoning considerations, but they become absolute in the psychology of an agent. The notion of value can thus become a principle to organise the reasons an agent has to argue, justify or refute the outcomes of a decision-making process in complex scenarios [8,9].

When considered part of the life of a group and its members, values possess a prescriptive power. E.g. communicating that something has a value will indirectly affect the mind of a social agent. If norms mandate specific actions or states of the world (i.e. goals), values give the agents a reason for pursuing the goal (i.e. because it is "good"). Previous works have explored the connection between norms and agents' preferences proposing design principles to represent different personalities in normative reasoning [2] and different cultural effects at the population level [1].

2.2 Drives

Drives are a tool to represent the agent internal state. Although they lack the representational content proper of goals, drives can be useful to express agents' motivations. More precisely, drives tell us what an agent need—when a drive is out of balance the agent has a need to satisfy. Implementing drives with an activation level and a threshold, they can act as triggers for agent's actions: if the level falls below the threshold an alarm sets off, and the agent has the need to select from his actions' repertoire the response capable to obtain the changes in the environment that will bring his drive back to a safe state, i.e. his need is satisfied.

Most physiological drives respond to this description: when an organism feels, e.g., hunger it will look for food, the ingested food will bring its energy level up and its body will stop signalling hunger for some time. But other agent's needs can be adapted and implemented in this way. It's the case of social drives, like affiliation and belonging, or recognition and prestige, which, although more complex to be connected to a single body signal or feeling, are nonetheless fundamental sources of motivation for the agents' behaviour. Hence in the following we are going to abstract from the level of the body and we are going to treat all implicit sources of motivation—both individual and social needs—as drives.

Drives' Update Function. A drive is identified by an update function, which is used to determine its **activation level**:

$$D_{level} = \tanh(\beta(\alpha_1 x_1 + \ldots + \alpha_n x_n - k))$$

where:

$\alpha_i x_i$ are the features (x) of the agent's behaviour and/or his environment
    connected to the satisfaction of the drive, and their relative strength (α);
β determines the speed and direction of change of the drive's level;
k is a constant factor consumed every time unit.

The shape of the faction also ensures that the every factor x_i will only have a *marginal effect* on the updated level.

A drive is further characterised by a **threshold**, $D_{threshold} = [-1, 1]$, which is responsible for signalling the presence of a need to the agent every time that $D_{level} < D_{threshold}$.

Much like we can talk about achievement goals and maintenance goals [3], we can here distinguish between achievement drives and maintenance drives, or in the terminology adopted by Ron Sun and colleagues, *achievement-oriented* and *avoidance-oriented* drives [7]. The difference in the two types of drives is in how they are affected by agent's inaction. Achievement drives are used to represent dynamics in the internal state of the agent that tend to move away from an equilibrium point, unless the agent performs some action that is able to increase the activation level of the drive. Maintenance or avoidance-oriented drives work in the opposite way: in its natural state the drive is already satisfied. It is only when the agent acts or some change in the world's state occurs that the level of the drive decreases. An example of the first kind of drive would be, again, hunger; in the present model we would talk about achievement drives when $\beta > 0$. An example of avoidance-oriented drives would be safety, and in this model it would mean that $\beta < 0$.[1]

Conflicting Drives. Motivations derived from one drive can lead an agent to perform actions that are detrimental to another one of his drives. Many animals have to escape predators (safety drive) and get enough rest (sleep drive). Although generally humans have evolved past this problem, an example of conflicting drives might be found in the need to resist a delicious cake (hunger drive) and the goal to lose weight (prestige drive). The conflict between drives is captured by the model connecting the drives update function to different features of the state of the world brought about by the agent actions. The trade-off between connected drives is then reached inspecting the agents' values: the action promoting values that are relatively more important for the agent will be selected for execution, which in turn will feedback at the level of the drives changing their activation level accordingly (see Figure 1).

Drives' Satisfaction and Side-Effects. Just as one agent can have conflicting drives whose needs he has to compromise, in a multi-agent system the state of the world realised by one agent acting to satisfy his needs might, and often will, have side-effects for other agents in the same environment.

Side-effects are computed by linking the same behavioural or environmental feature x to the drives of two (or more) agents. Side-effects can be both positive or negative, and together they capture the complexity of cooperation and conflict in social interactions.

---

[1] In order to allow the drive activation level to change over time, it must hold that $\beta \neq 0$.

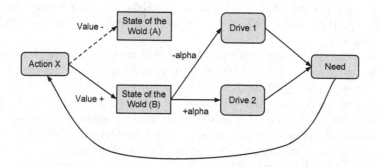

Fig. 1. Agents will compromise drive satisfaction if they can bring about a state of the world that is in line with their values

3 Simulation Scenario

To assess the performances of the developed model we are going to deploy and test it in the context of a simulation scenario. The scenario will centre around the dynamic of smoking behaviour in public places, like pubs and restaurants. The overall behaviour of the individual agents will be regulated by the level of four basic drives and the agents, who differ from each other in regard to their attitude towards smoking, will have to act in order to keep the highest number of drives in check. Output from two cultural groups, defined by the ordering of the agents' values, will be presented and used to analyse the features of the model.

The scenario explores a convivial situation and it assumes that all agents' actions, on top of directly affecting the agent's state, also carry a social meaning, consequently altering his affiliation with the rest of the agent. In simulating smoking behaviour we further assume the population to be divided in two subgroups, the smoker and the non-smokers, with conflicting interests. As described by Opp, "being exposed to smokers is an externality for many non-smokers. ... Non-smokers may control the externality by choosing the 'exit' option and changing places or by 'voice', such as asking the smoker to refrain from smoking or expressing anger for the annoyance. In this situation, a non-smoker P will have a *preference* that the smoker O will stop smoking." [6, pp. 133–134].

3.1 Implemented Drives and Values

We can capture this dynamic in the model by endowing the agents with a first pair of drives: (a) **nicotine**, controlling the need to smoke and (b) **tolerance**, that measures agents' dissatisfaction. The first drive has a *negative side-effect* on the tolerance of the other agents (smoking is an externality). And since the agents have two different preferences regarding smoking, they have different thresholds for the same drives: smokers have an extremely low threshold for *tolerance* and they will never feel the need to voice their dissatisfaction; non-smokers have an extremely low threshold for *nicotine* and they will never feel the need to light up a cigarette.

Agents in the present scenario have also two *conflicting drives*: (a) **affiliation**, controlling their sense of belonging and (b) **comfort**, a drive affected by the characteristics of the location of the agent. In our case, the agent's home is the location better suited to satisfy the need for comfort, but it is also the place where is less likely to meet other people. This way the agent decision to go out with friends is always made at the expenses of the comfort drive (and vice versa).

Since, as we said, all agents' actions carry a social meaning, we let the affiliation drive be conditionally affected also by choices made in the attempt to satisfy the nicotine or the tolerance drive. Smoking when in presence of a group of smokers, other than increasing the nicotine level, generates a positive feedback on the affiliation drive. As well as voicing disappointment against smokers in a group composed mainly of non-smokers generates a positive feedback on the affiliation drive of non-smoking agents.

The agents attitude towards smoking, and consequently the thresholds for the nicotine and tolerance drives, are derived from the values held by the agents and from those values' relative strength. Values and their strength is also used to guide the agents' decision-making every time their behaviour impacts on conflicting drives and their related needs. In the present scenario the agents hold the following values:

1. health: the realised benefits of healthy behaviours, together with the awareness of the risks associated with the negative consequences of being exposed to the unhealthy behaviour of others. .
2. hedonism: the general attitude to discount future consequences in favour of present rewards.
3. individualism: represents the extent to which agents identify with the group; how much the agents let their own behaviour be affected by shared ways of life.
4. equality: represents the importance agents attribute to differences in power, together with tendency to comply with the rules and obligations associated with the assigned roles.

The relative strength of the value of health and hedonism is responsible for the agents' attitude toward smoking: if hedonism is stronger than health, the agent will possess a positive attitude and, with a given percentage, he will be a smoker. In the cases where health is the stronger value the agents will belong to the non-smoking part of the population.

The relationship between the remaining two values is used experimentally to create two agents' cultures that are tested separately in the simulated model.

3.2 Agent's State and Simulation Cycle

Besides the four drives, their activation's levels and their thresholds, the values and their strength, an agent is described by three **individual variables**:

Algorithm 1. Simulation's main cycle

Result: Update agents' location, behaviour, and social response.

begin
    for $a \in agentList$ **do**
        if $a.Affiliation.inNeed() == a.Comfort.inNeed()$ **then**
            if $a.Individualism.strength > a.Equality.strength$ **then**
                | a.location = AtHome;
            else
                | a.location = ToThePub;
            end
        else
            if $a.Affiliation.inNeed()$ **then**
                | a.location = ToThePub;
            end
            if $a.Comfort.inNeed()$ **then**
                | a.location = AtHome;
            end
        end
    end
    for $a \in agentList$ **do**
        a.Behaviour = a.Nicotine.inNeed() ? Smoking : NonSmoking;
        if $a.location == ToThePub$ **then**
            if $a.Affiliation.inNeed()$ **then**
                if $a.isASmoker()$ **then**
                    | a.venue = a.$N_b > 1$? Outside : Inside;
                else
                    | a.venue = a.$N_s > 0.5$? Outside : Inside;
                end
            else
                | a.venue=Inside;
            end
        end
    end
    for $a \in agentList$ **do**
        if $a.location==ToThePub$ **and** $a.venue==Inside$ **then**
            if $a.Tolerance.inNeed()$ **then**
                if $a.Individualism.strength > a.Equality.strength$ **or**
                $!a.Affiliation.inNeed()$ **then**
                    | target = findSmokingAgent();
                    | a.Response = Voice;
                    | target.Response = Reproached;
                end
            end
        end
    end
    updateEnvironmentalVariables();
    for $a \in agentList$ **do**
        for $d \in a.Drives$ **do**
            | d.update();
        end
    end
end

1. **A location:** every agent can be either `AtHome` or `ToThePub`, meaning that he could be alone in his house and free to adopt the behaviour that he prefers; or in a public venue, possibly in the company of other agents.
2. **A behaviour:** either `Smoking` or `NonSmoking`, depending on the level of the nicotine drive and, depending on his affiliation's needs and whether he is in a public venue, he can decide to so either `Inside`—where other agents can react in a negative way at the presence of smokers—or `Outside`—meaning an outdoor venue, a place less comfortable, but where the other agents eventually present would not complain about Environmental Tobacco Smoke.
3. **A response:** depending on the location of the agent, his attitude on smoking, and the activation level of the tolerance drive, this variable could assume the value `Voice`, `Reproached`, or `null`. That is, a non-smoking agent can decide to voice his disappointment and ask a smoker to stop.

There is then a list of **environmental factors** resulting from the sum of the choices of the individual agents, which are monitored during the simulation and used, together with the above variables, to update the activation level of the agents' drives. These are:

N_a The number of *agents* in my environment, weighted against the size of the whole population and the number of venues accessible to the agents.

N_s The number of *smokers*, weighted against the number of agents in my environment.

N_v The number of complaining agents (*voicing*), relative to the number of agents in the same venue.

N_r The number of *reproached* agents, also relative to the total agents in the venue.

N_b The times an agent is being *blamed by voicing agents*.

Each simulation cycle an updated value for the three individual variables is computed by every agent in random order, the environmental variables updated and the level of the agents' drives consequently adjusted. The details are provided by Algorithm 1.

4   Results

To demonstrate the performance of the implemented model, in this section we present the output of three different simulations obtained exploring the space of the parameters of the drives' update function discussed in Subsection 2.2.

Results come from populations of 60 agents. We noticed that they are robust to changes in population's size. The number selected allows for a clearer graphical output. All the populations contain a group of agents labelled as `smokers`, determined by the value of hedonism being relatively more strong than the value of health and by a fixed percentage $p = 0.8$; all the rest are `non-smokers`. Smokers never voice disappointment: their $D_{threshold}$ for tolerance is set to -1.0. In a similar fashion, non-smokers never feel the need for smoking: their $D_{threshold}$

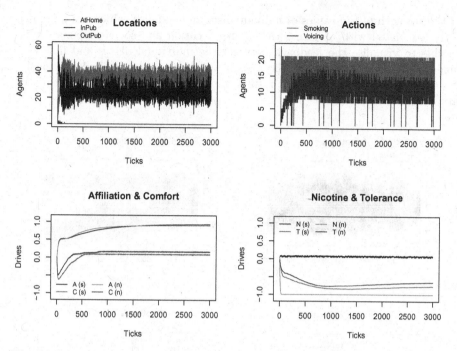

Fig. 2. Behavioural output (above) and average activation level of the four drives (below) for an agent population ($N = 60$) divided in smokers (s) and non-smokers (n), and where $Equality.strength > Individualism.strength$ (Egalitarian culture).

for nicotine is set to -1.0. Agents have their drives' activation level set up at a random value at the beginning of the simulations. All the other parameters are set up according to the following table:

	β	k	α_i	x_i	threshold
Nicotine	0.1	0.8	1.5	Smoking	0.0
Tolerance	-0.01	0.4	6.0	N_s	0.2
Comfort	-0.1	0.4	0.9	InThePub	0.4
Comfort			0.9	Outside	
Comfort			1.1	N_b	
Affiliation	0.01	0.4	3.0	N_a	0.5

Where nicotine and affiliation are implemented as achievement-oriented drives, while tolerance and comfort are avoidance-oriented. The absolute values of β ensures that nicotine and comfort, as needs, are experienced with a higher frequency by the agents. Nicotine is also a costly reward to abstain from. Conversely, affiliation and tolerance work at a much lower speed, giving the time to the agents to absorb changes in the (social) environment.

Defining parameters according to these criteria determines a behavioural pattern that is able to address a higher number of agents' needs. Controlling also for the strength of the values of individualism and equality, which are more directly associated with updating the agents' location and social response, it is possible to visualise the feedback between the individual drives and how the same structural asymmetry in the agents' preferences—as recalled previously from Opp—can generate different results when associated with a different motivational state.

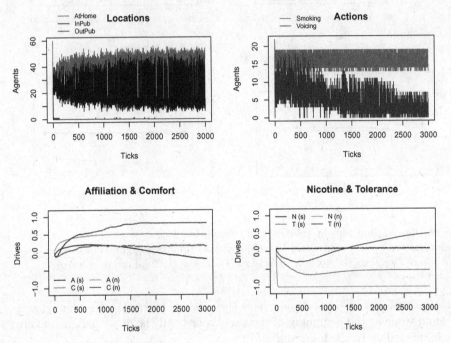

Fig. 3. Behavioural output (above) and average activation level of the four drives (below) for an agent population ($N = 60$) divided in smokers (s) and non-smokers (n), and where *Individualism.strength* > *Equality.strength* (Individualistic culture)

The results in Figure 2, where equality as a value is more important, leads to a behavioural pattern that can be characterised as gregarious, catering to the affiliations drives of the agents, but to the expenses of the non-smoking sub-group, which, regardless of their being vocal are not able to get rid of the annoyances of second-hand smoke, i.e. their tolerance activation level never reaches the threshold.

In the case of a stronger individualism value, Figure 3 shows a different pattern, in which the location of the agents changes more rapidly every simulation cycle, the number of complaining non-smoker tend to decrease over time, but the contrasting needs of the two sub-groups of agents plays out differently, with the tolerance level of the non-smokers improving at the expenses of the affiliation level of the smokers.

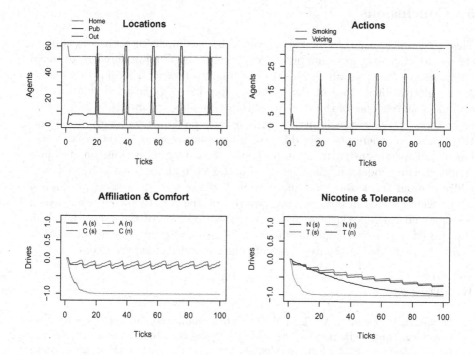

Fig. 4. Different initialization of the drives' update functions. Others variables as in Fig. 3.

Figure 4, finally, illustrates the performances of the system under extreme circumstances. The results are produced initialising the parameters with the set up of the following table:

	β	k	α_i	x_i	threshold
Nicotine	0.2	0.8	0.7	Smoking	0.0
Tolerance	-0.2	0.02	1.0	N_s	0.2
Comfort	-0.2	0.1	0.9	InThePub	0.0
Comfort			0.9	Outside	
Comfort			0.1	N_b	
Affiliation	0.2	0.8	0.5	N_a	0.5

Although less realistic, the displayed pattern is still logical and for this harsh definition of the parameters the algorithm still try to satisfy the agents' needs by keeping them home most of the time and moving them to a public venue only when the comfort activation level is well above the threshold. The brief interaction in the venue are not enough to satisfy the agents' need for affiliation, whilst giving the opportunity to the non-smoking agents to immediately reproach the smokers. The randomisation of the initial value of D_{level} here has been avoided to make the result more evident.

5   Conclusions

The system has proved to be responsive to changes in the motivational state of the agents. This feature is important for linking individual preferences to social outcomes. We have shown through our simulation how a structural asymmetry in the motivational state of the agent can produce significant changes in the overall social response of the system. This feature appears promising and pushes us to investigate the possibility of applying this model to the study of normative behaviour where not only different individual interests might be at stake, but higher social constructs are in play, such as obligation, permission, and prescription. Our model will allow us to go back to the analysis made by Opp and address in our framework the difference he highlights between *personal interest* of the agent, which in our case was covered by the negative feedback between nicotine and tolerance drives, and a *regulatory interest* of the agent, which in turn would require the implementation of elements of normative reasoning that should be grounded in the dynamics of values and drives we presented.

References

1. Dechesne, F., Dignum, V., Tan, Y.-H.: Understanding compliance differences between legal and social norms: The case of smoking ban. In: Dechesne, F., Hattori, H., ter Mors, A., Such, J.M., Weyns, D., Dignum, F. (eds.) AAMAS 2011 Workshops. LNCS (LNAI), vol. 7068, pp. 50–64. Springer, Heidelberg (2012)
2. Dignum, F., Dignum, V.: Emergence and enforcement of social behavior. In: Anderssen, R.S., Braddock, R.D., Newham, L.T.H. (eds.) 18th World IMACS Congress and MODSIM 2009 International Congress on Modelling and Simulation, pp. 2942–2948 (July 2009), http://www.mssanz.org.au/modsim09/H4/dignum.pdf
3. Duff, S., Harland, J., Thangarajah, J.: On proactivity and maintenance goals. In: Proceedings of the Fifth International Joint Conference on Autonomous Agents and Multiagent Systems, AAMAS 2006, pp. 1033–1040. ACM, New York (2006), http://dx.doi.org/10.1145/1160633.1160817
4. Hansson, S.O.: The Structure of Values and Norms. Cambridge Studies in Probability, Induction and Decision Theory. Cambridge University Press (July 2001)
5. Miceli, M., Castelfranchi, C.: A Cognitive Approach to Values. Journal for the Theory of Social Behaviour 19(2), 169–193 (1989)
6. Opp, K.D.: When do norms emerge by human design and when by the unintended consequences of human action? the example of the no-smoking norm. Rationality and Society 14(2), 131–158 (2002)
7. Sun, R.: Motivational representations within a computational cognitive architecture. Cognitive Computation 1(1), 91–103 (2009), http://dx.doi.org/10.1007/s12559-009-9005-z
8. van der Weide, T.: Arguing to Motivate Decisions. Ph.D. thesis, Utrecht University (2011)
9. van der Weide, T.L., Dignum, F., Meyer, J.-J.C., Prakken, H., Vreeswijk, G.A.W.: Practical reasoning using values. In: McBurney, P., Rahwan, I., Parsons, S., Maudet, N. (eds.) ArgMAS 2009. LNCS (LNAI), vol. 6057, pp. 79–93. Springer, Heidelberg (2010), http://dx.doi.org/10.1007/978-3-642-12805-9_5

Modeling the Propagation of Public Perception across Repeated Social Interactions

Taranjeet Singh Bhatia, Saad Ahmad Khan, and Ladislau Bölöni

Dept. of Electrical Engineering and Computer Science
University of Central Florida
4000 Central Florida Blvd, Orlando FL 32816
{tsbhatia,skhan,lboloni}@eecs.ucf.edu

Abstract. In this paper we develop an operational, quantitative method for the propagation of public perception. The model is presented as an extension of the culture-sanctioned social metric framework. We use the technique to model an extended version of the Spanish Steps flower selling scam, where a seller manipulates the belief of the clients and the public perception to pressure the clients to buy overpriced flowers.

1 Introduction

Humans are social beings. Even when pursuing selfish goals, they need to consider the impact of their actions on their public and peer perception. A simple model would only consider public perception as an *output* of the actions of the agents, for instance, a measure of their popularity. The reality, however, is different: the public perception is also an *input* into the actions of the agents: a "popular" agent can get away with actions which are out of reach to an "unpopular" one. Sometimes the *belief* of public perception is sufficient to affect actions - an agent which only believes itself to be popular will act as if it would be popular in reality.

The objective of this paper is to develop an operational, quantitative model for the propagation of public perception. It is part of our ongoing work with regards to modeling autonomous robots acting in social and cultural contexts [9,8,3]. The goal is to have a model which has explanatory power (why did the human act the way it did?), predictive power (how do we expect the human to act in a given situation?), and decision making power (how should a robot act in a given social setting?).

In [3] we have introduced the Spanish Steps scam, a scenario where the behavior of the participating humans can only be explained if we allow that they are simultaneously considering a number of factors, including financial gain or loss, loss of time and public and peer perceptions of dignity and politeness. We developed a modeling theory called the culture-sanctioned social metrics (CSSM) which allows us to perform an explanatory and predictive simulation of this scenario and other scenarios. CSSMs provide a relatively high-detail model of the social behavior: in its spirit, this technique falls close to the KIDS (Keep it Descriptive Stupid) approach advocated by Edmonds and Moss [6].

F. Giardini and F. Amblard (Eds.): MABS 2012, LNAI 7838, pp. 13–26, 2013.

The simulations where CSSMs had been deployed, however, up to this point were always considering a single interaction of several minutes at a time. However, the public perception can evolve over longer time frames spanning multiple interactions. Some of the most intriguing questions of public perception modeling are how the knowledge of individual actions propagates in space and time, how interactions at different spatio-temporal locations affect each other through the public perceptions and how does the general public (such as a crowd of bystanders) forms and forgets a public perception.

The work described in this paper extends the CSSM model towards the modeling of the propagation of public perception across multiple social interactions. For a concrete example, we will use an extended version of the Spanish Steps scenario which follows the interaction of a seller with multiple clients over a longer period of time. We make an effort to realistically model the public perception as provided by the ever changing crowd at a tourist attraction.

The remainder of this paper is organised as follows. The mechanism of the Spanish Steps scenario for an isolated instance of single seller/single client case is outlined in Section 2. Then, in Section 3 we discuss the mechanisms for multitasking from the point of view of the seller: how can the seller interleave the actions of multiple selling scenarios? How does the knowledge and beliefs propagate among the clients of the same seller? We show the results of an experimental study in Section 4 and discuss related work in Section 5.

2 The Analysis of an Isolated Spanish Steps Scenario

The Spanish Steps scenario is a flower selling scam perpetrated in many touristic sites across Italy, such as the Spanish Steps in Rome[1]. The intention of the seller is to pressure a client (typically a woman or a romantic couple) to purchase a rose at an inflated price:

- The seller offers a bouquet of flowers to the client. The client declines to purchase.
- The seller offers a single flower, relying on gestures implying that it is a gift. If the client refuses to take the flower, he repeats the offer several times, pushes the flower into the client's hands, or inserts it into her bag.
- The seller waits for 15-60 seconds several steps away from the client, who assumes that the interaction had concluded.
- The seller approaches the client and requests payment.
- The client attempts to return the flower. The seller refuses to take it. The action concludes by either the client paying or by escalating her verbal efforts to return the flower until the seller decides to take it back.

Let us now consider the ways in which this scenario can turn out. Real world observations of the scenario show that the scam sometimes succeeds *i.e.* the seller is able to make a sale and sometimes it fails: the client escalates her efforts

---

[1] A closely related scam is perpetrated by water-sellers in traditional costume in the Sultanahmet area in Istanbul.

to return the flower until the seller, begrudgingly, accepts it. A purely rational model centered on financial gain cannot explain the cases when the client buys the flower, well knowing that she is cheated. It also does not explain the cases when, in other situations, the seller abandons his high pressure selling tactic and accepts the return of the flower.

In our recent work, we argued that the participants in such transactions do not consider only tangible values such as financial worth, but also a number of *culture-sanctioned social metrics* (CSSMs), such as politeness and dignity, seen from the perspective of the self, significant peers, or the public at large. These values are not fully independent (one would give up politeness when confronted with a large financial loss) but they are not linearly convertible into each other.

An important point of the theory is that the impact of the actions on the CSSMs do not depend only on the action itself, but also on the *public perception* as seen by the players. These public perceptions or, more exactly, the beliefs of the players about them are critical in the personal calculus of the social values. For instance, it is not considered undignified to expose a scammer, but one looses face if he reneges on a publicly accepted transaction.

A model of the Spanish Steps scam using this model is described in [3]. The critical step is the manipulation of the public perception, such that the client will perceive herself as reneging on an accepted transaction. If this happens, then escalating the return of the flower will become very expensive in terms of dignity and politeness. The public knowledge of the crowd is critical to the success of the scam. The scam would never succeed in an empty street - as it relies on the reluctance of the client to lose dignity and perception of politeness by making a scene in public. Ironically, the best strategy of the client also relies on the public perception - if the client commands the sympathy of the crowd, she can escalate her efforts to return the flowers.

In this section, we describe the way in which an individual instance of the Spanish Steps scenario can be modeled and analyzed in the CSSM framework. The participants are the seller, the client and the general public. We will consider the client to be one member of a romantic couple, who also needs to consider the peer values from the point of view of his partner. We need to consider the action-state graph (with its associated detail variables), the culture-sanctioned social metrics and beliefs and public perceptions of the agents.

2.1   The Action-State Graph

The unfolding of the Spanish Steps scam can be relatively well separated in discrete steps, allowing us to draw an action-state graph as shown in Figure 1. This graph is not a full description of the interaction, only an aid in organizing our representations. Being in a certain node does not fully represent the state of the scenario - we need also to consider a number of *detail variables*. For instance, S6 is a state where the client holds the flower and had just attempted to return it to the seller. The details of this state include the judgment by the seller and the client of the current situation, as well as their emotional state. If the client believes that the public assumes that she had already accepted the transaction, she will be more reluctant to force the return.

Similarly, the actions represented by the edges of the graph are also parametrized by detail variables. In our model, A7, A9, and A16 are parametrized by their "loudness" x which determines how many onlookers will overhear the transaction and their "offensiveness" y which will determine how the action will impact the values of the actor and target of the action. The action A14 is parametrized with the waiting time t it involves.

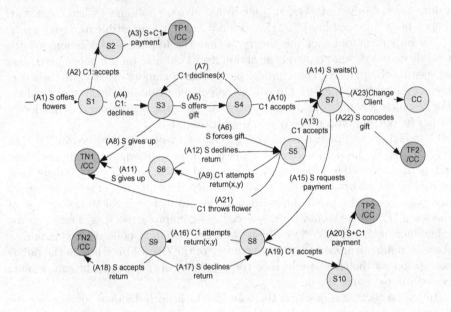

Fig. 1. The action-state graph of the Spanish Steps scam. The states marked with CC allow for the change of clients.

2.2   Culture-Sanctioned Social Metrics

Our modeling technique assumes that the agents explicitly maintain a vector of *metrics*, separated in two classes. *Concrete* metrics such as financial worth or time are easily measurable and come with their native measurement units (*e.g.* dollar or euro for financial worth, seconds or minutes for time). The second class of metrics are *intangibles*, which we model with culture-sanctioned social metrics (CSSMs). We say that a culture *sanctions* a metric if (a) has a name for it, (b) provides an (informal) algorithm for its evaluation, (c) expects its members to continuously evaluate these metrics for themselves and salient persons in their environment and (d) provides rules of conduct which depend on these metrics.

To model the Spanish Steps scenario we used two concrete metrics: the *financial worth* W and the *time* T and two CSSMs: the *dignity* D and the *politeness* P. Both sides consider the metrics from the perspective of the self and the public; the client also considers a peer (the other member of the romantic couple). With these assumptions, the vector of metrics for the client is $\{W^c, T^c, D^c, D_p^c, D_r^c, P^c, P_p^c, P_r^c\}$ while the vector of the seller is $\{W^s, T^s, D^s, D_p^s, P^s, P_p^s\}$.

2.3   Beliefs and Public Perceptions

Every action of an actor impacts the metrics of his own and his interaction partner. The change in a specific metric, by a specific action, in specific circumstances is given by the *action impact function* (AIF). Let us now investigate mathematical form of AIF. In the first approximation, the AIF depends on the detail parameters of the action. Let us consider action A16 (client attempts return), which is characterized by the *loudness* x and *offensiveness* y. Obviously, the higher these values, the stronger the effect on the dignity of the seller and the politeness and dignity of the client.

However, the impact also depends on the *beliefs of the public perception* of the scene. For a given level of loudness and offensiveness, it is less of a loss of dignity to be offensive with a crooked merchant than with an honest one. Similarly, one looses more dignity when reneging an agreed-upon transaction compared to correcting a misunderstanding.

As the agents do not have direct access to the public perception, we need to model the impact of public perception through their beliefs. Our modeling approach relies on the use of the Dempster-Shafer theory of evidence [15,16]. Events witnessed by the public are acting as evidence and are integrated using the *Dempster-Shafer conjunctive merge*. While we will use the belief component of the Dempster-Shafer model for our belief in public perception values, we will also retain the plausibility component which helps us estimate the uncertainty associated with a belief.

To model observed behavior of the real world players in the Spanish Steps scenario, we need to consider at least the following beliefs:

B_{gift}^c the client's belief that seller intends the flower to be a gift
B_{agr}^c and B_{agr}^s the client's and, respectively, sellers belief that the general public thinks that a transaction had been agreed upon.
B_{agr}^{sc} the sellers estimate of B_{agr}^c

We consider a number of other beliefs in the scenario involving the periodic interaction of seller over longer span of time. These beliefs include

- B_{dec}^c the client's belief that the seller is deceptive, being a function of past experiences.
- B_{dec}^w the client's belief that the crowd perceives the seller as deceptive, dependent upon the visual or verbal communication with other agents in the crowd and by the cultural understanding of the place

Naturally, beliefs are not orthogonal: a certain action can be evidence or counter-evidence against more than one belief. Furthermore, the way in which beliefs propagate between the agents depend on many factors, including the temporal and spatial aspects of the scenario. Clients who are in close proximity have a higher probability of information sharing. A tourist who had spent some time in the location has a better knowledge about the seller's deception than a newly arrived crowd member.

3   Multitasking

The seller in the Spanish Steps scam can not execute more than one action at a time, even if it involves multiple clients. Furthermore, basic rules of social interaction, such as the necessity to maintain physical proximity and eye contact prevent the seller from arbitrarily switching between clients. However, the Spanish Steps scam has certain states where switching away from a client *is* possible, and in some cases, such as state S7, even desirable. Exploiting these states, the seller can handle multiple simultaneous transactions, each in a specific state.

As the seller interacts physically with the clients, the clients will necessarily be in close physical proximity, and they will also likely be paying attention to the seller. Thus, we can make the assumption that the events unfolding in the parallel threads will be known to all the participants, and influence their beliefs.

To model the actions of the seller, we have designated some of the states in the state-action graph in Figure 1 as *change client* (CC) states. These are states where the seller has the possibility to either start a new interaction, by approaching a new client, or to resume the interaction with an existing client. Naturally, all the terminal states of the graph are CC states - in this case the interaction is terminated and the seller does not need to return to the client. State S7/CC, however, is not a terminal state: the seller will need to return to the client holding the flower.

Fig. 2-a shows the flow of three instances of the scenario where transitions are only made at terminal states. We call this a *serial interaction*. A serial interaction is not equivalent to three separate scenarios. While there is no overlap between the scenarios, there is a leak of information from one scenario to the next. This happens through two mechanisms: (a) through the clients in the later scenarios directly witnessing the outcomes of the previous scenarios, and (b) through the impact of the scenarios on the public perception.

Fig. 2-b shows an example where the seller *interleaves* the interaction with three different clients. In this case, the close physical proximity guarantees that the clients are aware of the unfolding of the scenario with the other clients. One would think that more information would help the clients, but this is not necessarily the case: the received information can actually be deceptive. The seller can actually derive an advantage from multitasking, beyond the purely time saving aspect. Let us consider the case of client C3 when entering the scenario, at state S1. For the sake of simplicity, let us consider that C3 had witnessed the evolution of the scenario of C1 and C2. In the scenario described

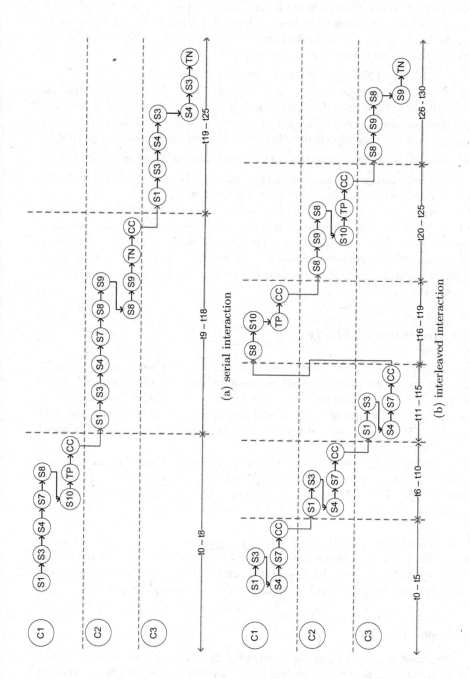

Fig. 2. Two techniques for handling multiple clients in the Spanish Steps scenario

in Fig. 2-a, C3 had seen the complete unrolling of the scenario two times. She knows that the single flower offered is not a gift, as she had seen the seller ask money for it on two different occasions. Thus C3, although she might choose to buy a bouquet of flowers, if she feels like it, will not fall for the scam, by not accepting the single flower from the seller. Her best choice is to take the path S4 $\xrightarrow{\text{A7(10)}}$ S3 $\xrightarrow{\text{A8}}$ TN1 out of the scenario.

In the scenario described in Fig. 2-b however, what C3 had seen is that the clients C1 and C2 accepted the single flower and had not been asked for money. This information would encourage C3 to accept the flower, and reach state S7 in the scenario. Note that the client will still be able to escape without paying by escalating the return efforts on the path of the repeated iterations of S8 $\xrightarrow{\text{A16(x)}}$ S9 $\xrightarrow{\text{A17}}$ S8 with increasing values of the parameter x. However, this will be vastly more expensive in terms of time, dignity and politeness.

If the seller does not interleave the clients, his best choice is to pause between the instances for a sufficiently long time such that the client C3 would not have witnessed the previous scenario. Alternatively, the seller might choose a client who had recently arrived to the scene. One way to achieve this is to move to a different location, to make sure that the bystanders have not witnessed the previous scenario.

4   Experimental Study

In the following we will describe a series of experiments which model the propagation of the public perception across multiple instances of the Spanish Steps scenario. The CSSM model had been implemented in the YAES simulation environment [4]. The Dempster-Shafer model had been implemented using the JDS library [17]. The simulation had been connected to a visual representation based on OpenWonderLand [18].

We have traced the model in three different scenarios. Each of them represent the activities of a seller enacting the Spanish Steps scam with three different clients C1, C2 and C3. The three experiments are described in Table 1.

Experiment 1 is an example of a serial interaction with no breaks between the scenarios. As soon as the seller finishes a scenario, he immediately chooses the next client and starts the next scenario. Experiment 2 is a serial interaction with breaks (delays) between the scenarios. To model the effect of the break, we have applied the Ebbinghaus forgetting curve to all the beliefs of the agents (essentially pulling the Dempster-Shafer values towards ignorance).

4.1 B_{gift} and D_p^s

In Experiment 1 the seller was successful with the first client, as he succeeded to raise B_{gift} from 0.5 to 0.8. The second and third clients, however, had witnessed this interaction, thus their own B_{gift} values had started from much lower values. In the case of C3, for instance, the B_{gift} value starts at 0.3. This is so low

Table 1. Experiments

Clients	Actions	Transaction
Experiment 1: Serial without breaks		
C1	$\xrightarrow[t0]{A1}$ S1 $\xrightarrow[t1]{A4}$ S3 $\xrightarrow[t2]{A5}$ S4 $\xrightarrow[t3]{A10}$ S7 $\xrightarrow[t4]{A15}$ S8 $\xrightarrow[t5]{A19}$ S10 $\xrightarrow[t6]{A20}$ TP2 $\xrightarrow[t7]{A24}$ CC	pass
C2	$\xrightarrow[t8]{A1}$ S1 $\xrightarrow[t9]{A4}$ S3 $\xrightarrow[t10]{A5}$ S4 $\xrightarrow[t11]{A10}$ S7 $\xrightarrow[t12]{A15}$ S8 $\xrightarrow[t13]{A16(0.2,0.2)}$ S9 $\xrightarrow[t14]{A17}$ S8 $\xrightarrow[t15]{A16(0.4,0.4)}$ S9 $\xrightarrow[t16]{A18}$ TN2 $\xrightarrow[t17]{A24}$ CC	fail
C3	$\xrightarrow[t18]{A1}$ S1 $\xrightarrow[t19]{A4}$ S3 $\xrightarrow[t20]{A5}$ S4 $\xrightarrow[t21]{A7(0.6,0.3)}$ S3 $\xrightarrow[t22]{A6}$ S5 $\xrightarrow[t23]{A9(0.5,0.5)}$ S6 $\xrightarrow[t24]{A11}$ TN1	fail
Experiment 2: Serial with breaks		
C1	$\xrightarrow[t0]{A1}$ S1 $\xrightarrow[t1]{A4}$ S3 $\xrightarrow[t2]{A5}$ S4 $\xrightarrow[t3]{A10}$ S7 $\xrightarrow[t4]{A15}$ S8 $\xrightarrow[t5]{A19}$ S10 $\xrightarrow[t6]{A20}$ TP2 $\xrightarrow[t7]{A14(20)}$ TP2 $\xrightarrow[t8]{A24}$ CC	pass
C2	$\xrightarrow[t9]{A1}$ S1 $\xrightarrow[t10]{A4}$ S3 $\xrightarrow[t11]{A5}$ S4 $\xrightarrow[t12]{A10}$ S7 $\xrightarrow[t13]{A15}$ S8 $\xrightarrow[t14]{A16(0.1,0.1)}$ S9 $\xrightarrow[t15]{A17}$ S8 $\xrightarrow[t16]{A19}$ S10 $\xrightarrow[t17]{A20}$ TP2 $\xrightarrow[t18]{A14(30)}$ TP2 $\xrightarrow[t19]{A24}$ CC	pass
C3	$\xrightarrow[t20]{A1}$ S1 $\xrightarrow[t21]{A4}$ S3 $\xrightarrow[t22]{A5}$ S4 $\xrightarrow[t23]{A10}$ S7 $\xrightarrow[t24]{A15}$ S8 $\xrightarrow[t25]{A19}$ S10 $\xrightarrow[t26]{A20}$ TP2	pass
Experiment 3: Interleaved		
C1	$\xrightarrow[t0]{A1}$ S1 $\xrightarrow[t1]{A4}$ S3 $\xrightarrow[t2]{A5}$ S4 $\xrightarrow[t3]{A10}$ S7 $\xrightarrow[t4]{A24}$ CC	hold
C2	$\xrightarrow[t5]{A1}$ S1 $\xrightarrow[t6]{A4}$ S3 $\xrightarrow[t7]{A5}$ S4 $\xrightarrow[t8]{A10}$ S7 $\xrightarrow[t9]{A24}$ CC	hold
C3	$\xrightarrow[t10]{A1}$ S1 $\xrightarrow[t11]{A4}$ S3 $\xrightarrow[t12]{A5}$ S4 $\xrightarrow[t13]{A10}$ S7 $\xrightarrow[t14]{A24}$ CC	hold
C1	$\xrightarrow[t15]{A15}$ S8 $\xrightarrow[t16]{A19}$ S10 $\xrightarrow[t17]{A20}$ TP2 $\xrightarrow[t18]{A24}$ CC	revisited/pass
C2	$\xrightarrow[t19]{A15}$ S8 $\xrightarrow[t20]{A16(0.3,0.3)}$ S9 $\xrightarrow[t21]{A17}$ S8 $\xrightarrow[t22]{A19}$ S10 $\xrightarrow[t23]{A20}$ TP2 $\xrightarrow[t24]{A24}$ CC	revisited/pass
C3	$\xrightarrow[t25]{A15}$ S8 $\xrightarrow[t26]{A16(0.3,0.3)}$ S9 $\xrightarrow[t27]{A17}$ S8 $\xrightarrow[t28]{A16(0.3,0.3)}$ S9 $\xrightarrow[t29]{A18}$ TN2	revisited/fail

that it allows the client to reject the offered single flower with high loudness and offensiveness values, which terminates the interaction (unsuccessfully for the seller) at state TN1.

Fig. 3a and Fig. 3b show the evolution of B_{gift} and the seller's public dignity D_p^s for Experiment 1.

In the second experiment, the seller performs the same scam, but this time he takes a break between the individual clients. This break guarantees that the clients did not see the unfolding of the previous scenarios, and the public perception had also returned to neutral. This is a result of both the gradual turnover of people in the crowd of the tourist attraction, and the natural forgetting of the individuals. As a result, all the clients are essentially starting from a neutral point. In Experiment 2 the seller had been successful in scamming all three clients. Naturally, we can have instances where a client would be able to avoid being scammed in this case as well, by escalating the loudness and offensiveness of her return efforts. However, even if she avoids the scam, the client will loose significant amount of dignity and politeness CSSMs, because she does not have the favorable support of the public. Fig. 3c and Fig. 3d show the evolution of B_{gift} and D_p^s for Experiment 2. Note, however, that taking long breaks is not an efficient way for the seller to maximize his profit W^s.

Experiment 3 shows an example of interleaved scenario. In this case, the clients are in close proximity, and aware of each other. However, up to state S7 neither they, nor the general public will be aware of the full flow of the scenario, thus they will actually have a higher B_{gift} then the two previous cases. On the other hand, once the seller starts to ask the clients for money, this information is quickly propagated to the remaining clients and the public perception as well. As a result, the public perception will gradually shift against the seller, eventually reaching the point where, in our experiment, client C3 can avoid being scammed, without significant loss of politeness and dignity. Fig. 3e and Fig. 3f show the evolution of B_{gift} and the seller's public dignity D_p^s for Experiment 3.

4.2 B_{dec}^c and B_{dec}^w

Fig. 4a and 4b shows the modeled values of of B_{dec}^c of clients and the evolution of B_{dec}^w for Experiment 1.

In Experiment 1, client C1 recognizes the seller's deception after time t=5, which raises B_{dec}^c to 0.5. As until time t5 the B_{dec}^w value is zero, C1 is not aware of the deception (which will be the ultimate cause of her buying the flower. Clients C2 and C3 recognize the seller's deception through the increase of their respective value of B_{dec}^w to 0.3. At time t=12 client C2 already has $B_{\text{dec}}^w \approx 0.5$ and $B_{\text{dec}}^c \approx 0.5$, which helps him reject those transactions in which the seller was loud and offensive.

Similarly, when the seller approaches client C3, she already knows about the deception with $B_{\text{dec}}^w \approx 0.7$, acquired from information from surrounding environment. This helps her reject the offer of the gift and avoid any communication with the seller. However, we can observe that the B_{dec}^c of client C3 decreases by 0.05 due to the fact that client had no personal interaction with the seller due to which the decision was solely based upon the information gathered from environment.

In Experiment 2, the seller waited 20 minutes before approaching the next client. This delay helps the seller to lower the B_{dec}^w. Although the client C2 has high B_{dec}^c as shown in Fig. 4c, he does not have sufficient B_{dec}^w (0.3) as shown in Fig. 4d to reject the offer publicly. The client C1 has no prior knowledge of seller's deception till time step t3 but after time step t7 this B_{dec}^c is not taken into consideration by other client's B_{dec}^w.

In Experiment 3, C1, C2 and C3 are not aware of the deception, having $B_{\text{dec}}^c = 0$ and $B_{\text{dec}}^w = 0$ until t=15 when the seller is asking C1 for money. Although C1 had witnessed the interaction of the seller with other clients, he had not seen any evidence of deception. Without having the support of the crowd in marking the seller as deceptive, C1 has no argument to reject the payment asked by seller. On the other hand, seeing this, C2 and C3 are rapidly raising their B_{dec}^c and B_{dec}^w values. Client C2 estimates $B_{\text{dec}}^w \approx 0.3$ when asked for the money. However, she judges this as an insufficent support for the crowd to escalate the effort to return the flower. On the other hand, C3 will have a value $B_{\text{dec}}^w \approx 0.7$ when asked for the money at t=23 as shown in Fig. 4e. This gives her sufficient confidence on the crowd's support to turn down the seller's offer. Thus, by the end of this interaction, the crowd became aware of the seller's deception. This is also depicted by the loss of the seller dignity D_p^s as shown in the Fig. 3f.

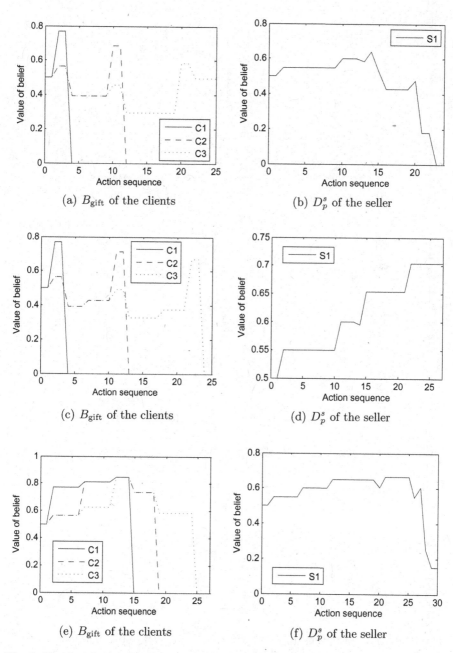

(a) B_{gift} of the clients

(b) D_p^s of the seller

(c) B_{gift} of the clients

(d) D_p^s of the seller

(e) B_{gift} of the clients

(f) D_p^s of the seller

Fig. 3. Non-interleaving without breaks (top row), Non-interleaving with breaks (middle row), Interleaving clients (bottom row)

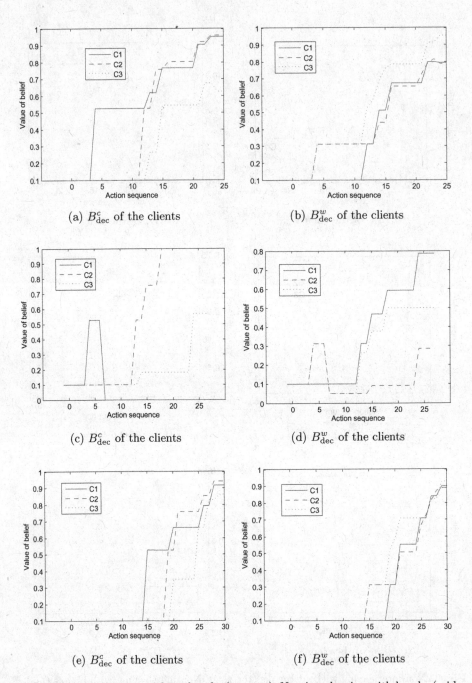

(a) B^c_{dec} of the clients

(b) B^w_{dec} of the clients

(c) B^c_{dec} of the clients

(d) B^w_{dec} of the clients

(e) B^c_{dec} of the clients

(f) B^w_{dec} of the clients

Fig. 4. Non-interleaving without breaks (top row), Non-interleaving with breaks (middle row), Interleaving clients (bottom row)

5   Related Work

Modeling the information propagation in human societies is a research area which had gathered a significant momentum in recent years. One foundation of this momentum is the development of network science [2] which provides a theoretical foundation for many of the information propagation models. From a practical point of view, computer supported social networks such as Facebook and Google+ have made available large amounts of statistical data, and the financial motivation to analyze it. Well documented examples of information propagation such as the organization of political demonstrations through instant messaging and Twitter had underscored the power and importance of this type of communication. There is relatively less work concerning the more traditional way of propagation of information through direct sensory perception which is the case of our paper.

The literature being very large, we can only consider several representative examples. Kottonau and Pahl-Wostl [10] studied the evolution of political attitudes in response to political campaigns - while in earlier work they studied the problem of new product diffusion. C. Motani et al. [13] implemented a virtual wireless social network based on the information spread in real social network such as a marketplace. Gruhl et al. [7] and Adar et al. [1] analyzed the person-to-person information flow over blog space topic sharing. Recent analysis of Twitter followers by Cha et al. [5] had shown that the influence of user on the topic can be gained by a concerted effort over a long period of time and a large number of followers are not an assurance to fame.

A significant amount of research had been directed towards the epidemic propagation of information in social networks [14,11,12]. In these papers, the information spread is modeled as virus infection in computer networks.

Acknowledgements. The research reported in this document/presentation was performed in connection with Contract Number W911NF-10-2-0016 with the U.S. Army Research Laboratory. The views and conclusions contained in this document/presentation are those of the authors and should not be interpreted as presenting the official policies or position, either expressed or implied, of the U.S. Army Research Laboratory, or the U.S. Government unless so designated by other authorized documents.

References

1. Adar, E., Adamic, L.: Tracking information epidemics in blogspace. In: Proc. of 2005 IEEE/WIC/ACM International Conference on Web Intelligence, pp. 207–214. IEEE (2005)
2. Albert, R., Barabási, A.: Statistical mechanics of complex networks. Reviews of Modern Physics 74(1), 47 (2002)
3. Bölöni, L.: The Spanish Steps flower scam - agent-based modeling of a complex social interaction. In: Proc. of 11th Int. Conf. on Autonomous Agents and Multiagent Systems (AAMAS 2012) (June 2012)

4. Bölöni, L., Turgut, D.: YAES - a modular simulator for mobile networks. In: Proceedings of the 8-th ACM/IEEE International Symposium on Modeling, Analysis and Simulation of Wireless and Mobile Systems MSWIM 2005, pp. 169–173 (October 2005)
5. Cha, M., Haddadi, H., Benevenuto, F., Gummad, K.: Measuring user influence on twitter: The million follower fallacy. In: Proc. of the Fourth Int'l AAAI Conference on Weblogs and Social Media, pp. 10–17. ACM (2010)
6. Edmonds, B., Moss, S.: From KISS to KIDS – an 'Anti-simplistic' modelling approach. In: Davidsson, P., Logan, B., Takadama, K. (eds.) MABS 2004. LNCS (LNAI), vol. 3415, pp. 130–144. Springer, Heidelberg (2005)
7. Gruhl, D., Guha, R., Liben-Nowell, D., Tomkins, A.: Information diffusion through blogspace. In: Proc. 13th Internat. World-Wide Web Conference. ACM, New York (2004)
8. Khan, S.A., Singh, T., Bölöni, L.: Soldiers, robots and local population - modeling cross-cultural values in a peacekeeping scenario. In: Proc. of the 21th Behavior Representation in Modeling & Simulation (BRIMS) Conference (March 2012)
9. Khan, S.A., Singh, T., Parker, S., Bölöni, L.: Modeling human-robot interaction for a market patrol task. In: Proc. of the 25th International FLAIRS Conference (2012)
10. Kottonau, J., Pahl-Wostl, C.: Simulating political attitudes and voting behavior. Journal of Artificial Societies and Social Simulation 7(4) (2004)
11. Liu, Z., Hu, B.: Epidemic spreading in community networks. Europhys. Lett., epl 72, 315 (2005)
12. May, R., Lloyd, A.L.: Infection dynamics on scale-free networks. Phys. Rev. E 64(6), 066112 (2001)
13. Motani, M., Srinivasan, V., Nuggehalli, P.: PeopleNet: Engineering a wireless virtual social network. In: Proc. of ACM MobiCom 2005. ACM (2005)
14. Pastor-Satorras, R., Vespignani, A.: Epidemic spreading in scale-free networks. Phys. Rev. Lett. 86(14), 3200–3203 (2001)
15. Shafer, G.: A mathematical theory of evidence. Princeton University Press, Princeton (1976)
16. Yager, R.: On the Dempster-Shafer framework and new combination rules. Information sciences 41(2), 93–137 (1987)
17. JDS: Java Dempster-Shafer Library, http://sourceforge.net/projects/jds/
18. Open Wonderland 3D virtual world toolkit, http://openwonderland.org

Effects of Combined Human Decision-Making Biases on Organizational Performance

Silvia Berlinger and Friederike Wall

Controlling and Strategic Management,
Alpen-Adria-Universitaet Klagenfurt, 9020 Klagenfurt, Austria

Abstract. As extensive experimental research has shown individuals suffer from diverse biases in decision-making. In our paper we analyze the effects of decision-making biases of managers in collaborative decision processes on organizational performance. The analysis employs an agent-based simulation model which is based on the NK model. In the simulations, managerial decisions which are based on different levels of organizational complexity and different incentive systems suffer from biases known from descriptive decision theory. The results illustrate how biases in combination with each other and in different organizational contexts affect organizational performance. We find that, contrary to intuition, some combinations of biases significantly improve organizational performance while these biases negatively affect organizational performance when they occur separately. This might evoke considerations whether decision-making should be as rational as possible.

Keywords: Agent-Based Simulation, Decision-Making, Organization.

1 Introduction

According to Simon humans suffer from bounded rationality [1] and, in particular, experience severe difficulties solving complex decision problems.

We know from descriptive decision theory that human decision-making behavior is influenced by several biases such as the recency effect [2],the status quo bias [3], and the anchor effect [4]. The recency effect tells us that individuals are more likely to remember information received at a later time than information received previously. The status quo bias refers to the tendency to overweight the current performance state. According to the anchor effect individuals set a mental anchor on which they strongly rely.

A prominent research method to show the effect of biases is the experiment. In experimental research, biases are usually analyzed under controlled laboratory conditions. For example, Kahneman and Tversky [5] experimentally explored the effects of framed information by providing different formulations of decision problems to some test groups. The study indicates that the formulation is a significant concern for the choices made by the test subjects. However, it is a challenge to isolate the various biases from each other in order to examine the impact of the biases in specific situations and to analyze how biases in combination with each other affect decision-making.

F. Giardini and F. Amblard (Eds.): MABS 2012, LNAI 7838, pp. 27–42, 2013.
© Springer-Verlag Berlin Heidelberg 2013

An alternative way to analyze decision-making behavior are agent-based simulations [6–8]. Using this method it is possible to simulate a broad range of constellations of decision-making processes in organizations as well as human behavior in various characteristics and under various, though controlled conditions. In particular, agent-based simulation allows for mapping the organizations which encapsulate the delegation of decisional competencies and collaborative decision-making. Furthermore, this method allows for representing further elements of organizational design like incentive systems and coordination mechanisms. Both elements serve to align individual decision-making with the overall objective of the organization.

However, it is rather unlikely that a decision-maker in an organization suffers from one distinct bias only; instead we have to assume that several biases occur simultaneously. This leads us to the compelling research question of this paper: How do biases in combination with each other on the individual decision-makers site affect the achievement of the overall organizational objective?

In particular, we analyze the effects of some prominent decision-making biases on the performance of collaborative organizations. To control biases in different combinations and on different levels of complexity of collaborative decision-making we use an agent-based simulation based on the NK model [9, 10]. Furthermore, we vary the reward structure: given that decision-makers seek to maximize their individual utility in terms of compensation, we provide them different incentives and, by that, shape the decision-makers perspective when making their choices.

The remainder of the paper is organized as follows: The subsequent section presents the agent-based simulation model including the organizational structure with collaborative decision-making and the decision-making biases under investigation. In Section 3 the main results of our simulations are presented and discussed. The final section gives some concluding arguments and refers to further research work.

2 Agent-Based Simulation Model

The agent-based simulation model is based on the NK model as introduced by Kauffman [9, 10]. This model has been adopted to the analysis of organizations by many management scholars, e.g. [11–14], and used for analyzing decision-making with imperfect information [15]. However, to the best of our knowledge, the NK model has not yet been used for analyzing managerial decision-making against the background of distinct decision-making biases. In our simulation model the structure of the decision-making organization includes departments, competencies of decision-makers, and incentive systems. With respect to the organizational structure our model is similar to Siggelkow and Rivkin [13]. Beyond that, our decision-makers suffer from biases which we regard to be the distinctive feature of our model.

In prior research human biases have been modeled and implemented in several ways like in [16] who analyses the anchoring effect of consumer price negotiations within the bargaining-zone model (the bargaining zone is the difference between the buyer's and seller's reservation prices). Kant and Thiriot [17] describe a cognitive decision agent model, where the decision-makers are modeled in a multi-agent system. In this model the authors use agents with one specific bias for each agent for a simulation of a small experimental financial market. Furthermore, An [18] gives an overview of how to model human decisions in coupled human and natural systems within agent-based models, in which environmental consequences affecting future human decisions and behavior are analyzed. However, as far as collaborative decision-making is concerned, to the very best of our knowledge, agent-based modeling has not yet been applied. In order to represent biases we use findings from descriptive decision theory. We focus our study on three biases: the recency effect, the status quo bias and the anchor effect. All three biases have in common that they do not directly relate to human problems in estimating probabilities of uncertain events; instead these biases rather relate to decision-makers' preferences and perceptions of information. Thus, the very core of our simulation model is that collaborative decision-making processes with different combinations of biased decision-making managers is investigated on the basis of the NK model.

2.1   Organizational Structure

The organization in our model experiences a ten-dimensional binary decision problem d as in [15]. Thus, the managers make decisions $d_i \in \{0,1\}$ with $i = 1,\ldots,10$. As the simulation is based on Kauffman's NK model [9], the organizational performance corresponds to the fitness of the NK model. Within this model there exists a fitness landscape in which agents seek to improve their performance by moving from "fitness valleys" to higher "fitness peaks". In our model, N defines the number of decisions which the organizations have to make and $N = 10$. K denotes the level of interactions between the decisions. K can range from 0 to $N - 1$. In case of $K = 0$, the N decisions are uncorrelated in the fitness landscape and the landscape has one single peak. In case of $K = N - 1$ the interactions among decisions are raised to maximum and each decision affects the fitness (performance) of all other decisions. Each decision d_i provides a contribution C_i with $0 \leq C_i \leq 1$. C_i depends on the single decision d_i, but with regard to the level K of interactions of the ten-dimensional decision problem also on other decisions d_i^j with $j = 1,\ldots,K$. For simplicity, in our model the level K of interactions is the same for all decisions d_i. Hence, the performance contribution C_i is given by $C_i = f_i(d_i; d_i^1,\ldots,d_i^K)$. The value of f_i is randomly drawn from a uniform distribution from the unit interval, i.e., $U[0,1]$ to the overall performance $V(d)$. The overall organizational performance $V(d)$ results from

$$V(\boldsymbol{d}) = \frac{1}{N}\sum_{i=1}^{N} C_i = \frac{1}{N}\sum_{i=1}^{N} f_i(d_i; d_i^1,\ldots,d_i^K). \tag{1}$$

An organization consists of a main office and two departments. Each department has primary control over a subset of the ten decisions. In our model department 1 has the control over the first five decisions and department 2 controls the second five decisions.

In our model, the decision makers aim at improving performance. In particular, the timeline of the search process for higher levels of performance is segmented into periods and in each period the decision makers seek for a configuration that promises a higher performance than achieved in the previous period, i.e. with the the current configuration d. In each period a department head makes decisions in her/his "own" subset of decisions and chooses the best of three partial configurations available in that period. In particular, each department head discovers two alternative partial configurations and, hence, has three options to choose from, (1) the status quo, (2) an alternative with one place of the binary problem space changed and (3) another alternative configuration where two places of the binary problem space are altered.

Our model incorporates a rather decentral mode of coordination: Each department head chooses the partial configuration that promises the highest individual utility independent of the other department's choices. Furthermore, the main office does not intervene in decision-making. Consequently, the ten-dimensional configuration that is chosen and implemented in a period is the result of the two departmental choices. Hence, the role of the main office is limited to registering the departmental and the organizational performance realized at the end of each period and to compensating the department heads according to their performance.

As mentioned previously, the department heads seek to maximize compensation according to the incentives given. The incentive structure in our model corresponds to the model of Siggelkov and Rivkin [13]: Each department head is rewarded according to a linear incentive system. The incentive mode is controlled by the parameter INC_r. If INC_r is set to 0 only the departmental performance P_r^{own} is rewarded while while the residual performance $P_r^{residual}$ is considered in decision-making in case that $INC_r \succ 0$. If $INC_r = 1$, organizational performance is rewarded. Hence, the ranking of configuration d by department r is based on the value base $B_r(d)$ given by

$$B_r(d) = P_r^{own}(d) + INC_r * P_r^{residual}(d) \tag{2}$$

However, in case of cross-departmental interactions, choices of one department may affect the contributions of decisions the other department is in charge of and vice versa. Hence, it depends on the interaction structure whether a department head solely has control over the departmental performance (the "self" structure in our simulation model) or whether the other department's decisions affect the departmental performance (the "full"-interdependent structure), and, consequently, also the manager's compensation. In our model, we simulate two interaction structures of decisions, i.e. the "self"-contained and the "full"-interdependent structure. The "self"-contained structure represents the case where intradepartmental interactions among decisions are maximal intense while no cross-departmental interdependencies exist. The self-contained structure is mapped in Table 1. An "x"-entry indicates that contribution C_i is affected by decision d_j, an "-" indicates that no effect of decision d_j on contribution C_i exists. In the self-contained structure there are interactions between the "own" decisions only. In the "full"-interdependend structure all decisions affect the performance contributions of all other decisions as can be seen in Table 2, i.e., cross-departmental interactions are maximal.

Table 1. Self-contained structure

	d_1 d_2 d_3 d_4 d_5	d_6 d_7 d_8 d_9 d_{10}	
C_1	x x x x x	- - - - -	
C_2	x x x x x	- - - - -	
C_3	x x x x x	- - - - -	P^{own}
C_4	x x x x x	- - - - -	
C_5	x x x x x	- - - - -	
C_6	- - - - -	x x x x x	
C_7	- - - - -	x x x x x	
C_8	- - - - -	x x x x x	$P^{residual}$
C_9	- - - - -	x x x x x	
C_{10}	- - - - -	x x x x x	

Table 2. Full-interdependent structure

	d_1 d_2 d_3 d_4 d_5	d_6 d_7 d_8 d_9 d_{10}	
C_1	x x x x x	x x x x x	
C_2	x x x x x	x x x x x	
C_3	x x x x x	x x x x x	P^{own}
C_4	x x x x x	x x x x x	
C_5	x x x x x	x x x x x	
C_6	x x x x x	x x x x x	
C_7	x x x x x	x x x x x	
C_8	x x x x x	x x x x x	$P^{residual}$
C_9	x x x x x	x x x x x	
C_{10}	x x x x x	x x x x x	

2.2 Human Biases

The choices of the department heads described in the previous section are also affected by decision-making biases. As mentioned previously we selected three different biases known from descriptive decision theory for our current analysis as mentioned above: the recency effect, the status quo bias, and the anchor effect.

In our model the heads of the two departments might suffer from all of these biases. However, the intensity of the biases may vary. Furthermore, our model allows for providing to the managers different parameters characterizing the biases, but for the sake of simplicity every manager gets the same parameters in the same weights and combinations, i.e., suffers from the same biases with the same intensities. Each department head makes one choice in each period. In each period each department head discovers two alternative configurations of the partial decision vector he/she is in charge of. For simplification, we assume that the managers get to know these three configurations at random order. The biases come into effect when a department head compares the two newly discovered configurations and the status quo with each other. In particular, the department heads make their choices based on a *perceived* rather than the *actual* value base for compensation. The *perception* $\tilde{B}$ of the actual value base B for compensation (see formula 2) resulting from a certain configuration d is given by

$$\tilde{B}_r(d, n) = B_r(d) * (1 - ((x_{max} - X_{n,d}) * \alpha) + q + (\gamma * A) \tag{3}$$

The perceived value base for compensation is influenced by several parameters which are used to map the biases under investigation: $\alpha \in \{0, 0.05, 0.1, 0.15, 0.2\}$ is used to represent the recency effect. In our model the recency effect is represented in that the decision-maker perceives an option the less favorable the earlier he/she gets to know of that option. The incoming order at point of time n of a configuration d is mapped with $X_{n,d} \in \{1, 2, 3\}$. x_{max} denotes the maximum order of incoming configurations for rating and is set to $x_{max} = 3$, because there are three options in each decision-making period. By multiplying the actual order of the configuration for rating by the recency effect α with $((x_{max} - X_{n,d}) * \alpha)$ we are able to assign the adequate weighting to the configuration depending on the actual order. This means that an option which is shown to the decision-maker at last is weighted higher than an option incoming with number two or one (in this order).

For mapping the status quo effect we introduce the q parameter, with $q \in \{0, 0.05, 0.1, 0.15, 0.2\}$. If the configuration under assessment does not correspond with the status quo, q is set to zero; otherwise q influences the rating of the configuration. This means, if the configuration shown to the manager-agent is the status quo it is weighted with the bias strength.

The anchor effect is mapped by inserting γ, with $\gamma \in \{0, 0.05, 0.1, 0.15, 0.2\}$. It is weighted on the value base for compensation A of the very first configuration, that the managers know within the adaptive walk: The organization is randomly thrown in the performance landscape; in our model the randomly assigned initial position serves as an anchor for decision-making and, hence, influences the subsequent decisions in the search process. By adding $(\gamma * A)$ to the base a more or less intensive anchor effect is revealed corresponding to the level of intensity of γ.

In order to investigate the combined biases we consider a simple additive coherence of them and, hence, we get the term $(1 - ((x_{max} - X_{n,d}) * \alpha) + q + (\gamma * A))$ as indicated in formula 3. Finally, by multiplying the resulting bias intensity by the actual value for compensation related to the configurations $B_r(d)$ (corresponding to formula 3) that the department heads consider in a period it is possible to simulate the combined effects of the biases in decision-making on organizational performance.

3   Results and Interpretation

3.1   Parameter Settings

In our simulations artificial organizations are observed for 300 periods while searching for higher levels of organizational performance. The simulation starts from a randomly assigned initial position in the performance landscape. For each setting of parameters 1000 landscapes are generated with 5 search cycles on each. As mentioned above, our organizations either have a "self"-contained structure or show "full" cross-departmental interactions. With respect to the incentive scheme, in principle, INC_r could take all values in the interval from 0 to 1. However, in order to be clear and concise we find it helpful to restrict the results presented below to the most relevant reward systems. Therefore, we present results for $INC_r = 0$ where only departmental performance is rewarded and for $INC_r = 1$ meaning that firm-wide is rewarded. Furthermore, decision-makers are rewarded either on the basis of their departmental or on the basis of the firmwide performance (i.e., $INC_r = 0$ or $INC_r = 1$, respectively). The decision-making biases are simulated at various levels of intensity. For simplification we simulate bias-intensities between 0% and 20% in order to analyze different levels of distorted perceptions. Thus, bias-intensities range from 0 to 0.2 in steps of 0.05 for all biases under investigations. For examining the impact of the decision-making biases in combination with each other, we combine two of them.

3.2   Combination of the Recency Effect and the Status Quo Bias

Table 3 reports final performances for the combinations simulated under different interaction structures and incentives given (as far as single values are concerned the most interesting ones, as discussed below, are set in italics). We start our analysis with a self-contained organization by combining the recency effect with the status quo bias.

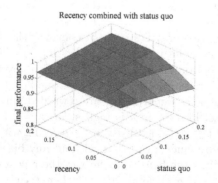

Fig. 1. Recency & status quo, self-contained, departmental incentives

In case that neither the recency effect nor the status quo bias are effective, i.e., $\alpha = 0$ and $q = 0$ (see Table 3), organizations achieve a high level of performance if departmental incentives are given. By intensifying the status quo bias the final performance decreases. However, the effects of the status quo bias on the final performance are apparently compensated by the recency effect (see Figure 1). Even for high levels of the status quo bias, the final performance increases continuously to a level achieved without any biases if the recency effect is more intense. In some combinations of bias intensities the final performance is even higher than without any biases. For $\alpha = 0.05$ and $q = 0.1$, performance is highest. Almost the same performance level was achieved by setting $\alpha = 0.1$ and $q = 0.15$, which yields nearly the same performance as if no biases occur. If the recency effect is effective only, the decrease in final performance is marginal. Figure 2 shows similar results for organizations that reward firm performance (i.e., $INC_r = 1$). The status quo bias causes a decrease in performance, whereas performance apparently increases with a more intense recency effect. In particular, performance is highest when $\alpha = 0.05$. But both effects in combination with each other lead to a much better performance at $q = 0.2$ with $\alpha = 0.1$ (Table 3).

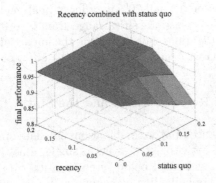

Fig. 2. Recency & status quo, self-contained, firmwide incentives

Using the same parameters as above but in the full-interdependent structure we revealed the following results: As shown in Figures 3 and 4 performance decreases when status quo bias is effective only. In contrast, the recency effect increases performance as long as its intensity is lower than $\alpha = 0.15$. Beyond that level of intensity final performance decreases. A higher level of intensity can be achieved by combining recency effect with status quo bias (see Figure 3). In this parameter constellation the departments are rewarded only on the basis of departmental performance. Performance is highest at $\alpha = 0.15$ with $q = 0$ and at $\alpha = 0.15$ with $q = 0.1$ (see Table 3). Even for $\alpha = 0.2$ with $q = 0.2$ the simulation shows higher performance levels than without any biases.

In case of firmwide incentives the beneficial effect of the recency bias in case of a status quo bias seems to be even more relevant: For example, in the full-interdependent structure in case that no recency effect is effective the losses of

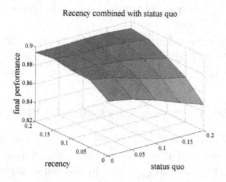

Fig. 3. Recency & status quo, full-interdep., departmental incentives

high status quo biases at a 0.2 level go up to more than 6 points of percentage compared to the situation of no status quo bias. With increasing recency effects these losses disappear.

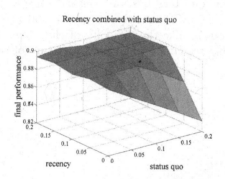

Fig. 4. Recency & status quo, full-interdep., firmwide incentives

Results indicate, that if managers are strongly influenced by the status quo bias, the adaptive walks do not lead to high performance levels. A high influence of the status quo bias in isolated conditions was found in [19], too. However, if managers underlie a strong status quo bias in combination with a strong recency effect, it is apparently possible to compensate the status quo bias or even achieve a higher performance level than without any biases.

In a way these results are not as surprising as they might appear at a first glance. In particular, hill-climbing algorithms are rather prone to inertia in case of highly rugged fitness landscapes: Then, the fitness landscape has many local maxima and the organizations are likely to stick to local maxima. With a status quo bias sticking to a current position is even more likely, since the status quo configuration is relatively overestimated compared to the alternative. The recency effect serves as a kind of countermeasure since it assures that eventually other alternatives than the status quo are overestimated. In this way, the recency effect increases the diversity of search.

In general, from analyzing these four constellations we can state, that biases may enfold beneficial effects and that performance depends on the way in which the status quo bias and the recency effect occur in combination with each other.

3.3   Combination of the Anchoring Effect and the Status Quo Bias

In our study we also analyzed the combined effects of the anchor effect and the status quo bias. As shown in Table 3 the anchor effect apparently does not enhance or mitigate the status quo bias, neither in the self-contained nor in the full-interdependent structure and regardless of the incentives given. For a given level of status quo bias our simulations yield similar levels of performance for all levels of the anchoring effect. Put the other way round, our study reveals a clear trend to lower performance if the status quo bias is intensified independendly of the anchoring effect. Results are illustrated in Figure 5 and Figure 6 for a self-contained structure and in Figure 7 and Figure 8 for a full-interdependent structure. By giving departmental incentives as well as firmwide incentive the results show that the status quo bias has a strong influence at every level of anchoring effect. A similar trend is found by Samuelson and Zeckhauser in [3] for diverse economic phenomena like the difficulty of changing public policies, preferred types of marketing techniques, and for the nature of competition in markets.

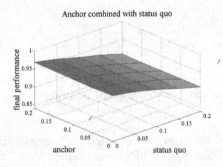

Fig. 5. Anchor & status quo, self-contained, departmental incentives

3.4   Combination of the Anchoring Effect and the Recency Effect

Finally, we investigated the recency and the anchor effect in combination with each other for the self-contained and the full-interdependent structure. Figures 9 and 10 show the results for departmental and firmwide incentives respectively in a self-contained structure. The plots show rather scattered patterns though at quite low performance differences as can also be seen in Table 3.

Table 3. Effects of biases in organizations with decentral coordination mode

	departmental incentives					firmwide incentives				
					self-contained					
	status quo									
recency	0	0.05	0.1	0.15	0.2	0	0.05	0.1	0.15	0.2
0	*0.97001*	0.95763	0.94221	0.92511	0.90749	0.96968	0.94475	0.91366	0.87884	0.84901
0.05	0.96911	*0.97025*	*0.97184*	0.96000	0.94474	0.97134	0.96929	*0.97081*	0.94595	0.91525
0.1	0.96950	*0.97019*	*0.97031*	*0.97100*	0.96932	0.97044	0.96802	0.96955	*0.97075*	*0.97135*
0.15	0.96876	0.96989	0.96895	0.96904	*0.97059*	0.96838	0.96901	0.96789	0.96819	0.97058
0.2	0.96975	0.96915	0.96941	0.96969	0.96835	0.96878	0.96823	0.96847	0.96972	0.96722
					full-interdependent					
	status quo									
recency	0	0.05	0.1	0.15	0.2	0	0.05	0.1	0.15	0.2
0	0.87904	0.87420	0.86641	0.85680	0.84794	*0.89469*	0.87883	0.86383	0.84821	*0.83166*
0.05	0.89223	0.88823	0.88042	0.87343	0.86759	0.89685	0.89705	0.89788	0.88312	0.86633
0.1	0.89314	0.89250	0.88938	0.88560	0.87935	0.89298	0.89572	0.89552	0.89674	0.89693
0.15	*0.89673*	0.89401	*0.89520*	0.89353	0.88985	0.89640	0.89629	0.89528	0.89517	0.89506
0.2	0.89423	0.89389	0.89478	0.89469	0.89256	*0.89410*	0.89726	0.89336	0.89511	*0.89413*
					self-contained					
	status quo									
anchor	0	0.05	0.1	0.15	0.2	0	0.05	0.1	0.15	0.2
0	0.96838	0.95813	0.94342	0.92517	0.90903	0.96968	0.94475	0.91366	0.87884	0.84901
0.05	0.96708	0.95696	0.94157	0.92712	0.90810	0.96891	0.94445	0.91279	0.88182	0.85124
0.1	0.96774	0.95812	0.94268	0.92579	0.90809	0.96994	0.94522	0.91212	0.88075	0.84883
0.15	0.96925	0.95769	0.94240	0.92535	0.90747	0.96998	0.94536	0.91243	0.88096	0.84852
0.2	0.96985	0.95817	0.94145	0.92728	0.90937	0.96741	0.94409	0.91262	0.87959	0.84809
					full-interdependent					
	status quo									
anchor	0	0.05	0.1	0.15	0.2	0	0.05	0.1	0.15	0.2
0	0.88188	0.87541	0.86650	0.85720	0.85121	0.89469	0.87883	0.86383	0.84821	0.83166
0.05	0.88281	0.87529	0.86669	0.85567	0.84982	0.89551	0.87971	0.86477	0.84716	0.83164
0.1	0.88135	0.87355	0.86540	0.85793	0.84839	0.89570	0.88013	0.86447	0.84637	0.83273
0.15	0.88088	0.87570	0.86783	0.85795	0.84801	0.89441	0.88115	0.86370	0.84658	0.83004
0.2	0.88090	0.87598	0.86684	0.85760	0.84673	0.89422	0.88090	0.86472	0.84613	0.83173
					self-contained					
	recency									
anchor	0	0.05	0.1	0.15	0.2	0	0.05	0.1	0.15	0.2
0	0.96838	0.97059	0.97084	0.96910	0.96839	0.96968	0.97134	0.97044	0.96838	0.96878
0.05	0.96708	0.96910	0.97114	0.96776	0.96988	0.96891	0.96965	0.96967	0.96875	0.96881
0.1	0.96774	0.96971	0.96886	0.97066	0.96912	0.96994	0.96971	0.97100	0.96897	0.96767
0.15	0.96925	0.96960	0.96969	0.96947	0.96973	0.96998	0.96939	0.97019	0.96889	0.96732
0.2	0.96985	0.96971	0.96983	0.97105	0.97069	0.96741	0.97001	0.96850	0.96925	0.96943
					full-interdependent					
	recency									
anchor	0	0.05	0.1	0.15	0.2	0	0.05	0.1	0.15	0.2
0	0.88188	0.89027	0.89473	0.89383	*0.89375*	0.89469	0.89685	0.89298	0.89640	0.89410
0.05	0.88281	0.89162	0.89296	0.89600	*0.89425*	0.89551	0.89394	0.89712	0.89564	0.89489
0.1	0.88135	0.88947	0.89370	0.89500	*0.89368*	0.89570	0.89649	0.89450	0.89750	0.89481
0.15	0.88088	0.89091	0.89225	0.89739	*0.89684*	0.89441	0.89595	0.89591	0.89465	0.89594
0.2	0.88090	0.89051	0.89462	0.89430	*0.89504*	0.89422	0.89673	0.89560	0.89639	0.89372

The confidence intervals vary between 0.006 and 0.007 for a confidence level of 0.001.

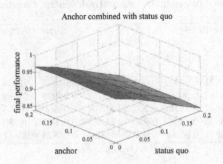

Fig. 6. Anchor & status quo, self-contained, firmwide incentives

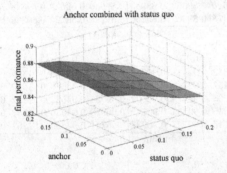

Fig. 7. Anchor & status quo, full-interdep., departmental incentives

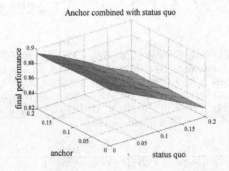

Fig. 8. Anchor & status quo, full-interdep., firmwide incentives

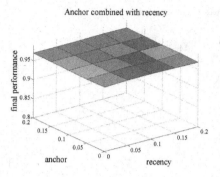

Fig. 9. Anchor & recency, self-contained, departmental incentives

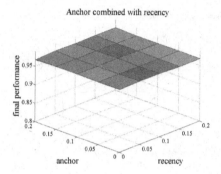

Fig. 10. Anchor & recency, self-contained, firmwide incentives

Figures 11 and 12 show the results for departmental and firmwide incentives respectively for the full-interdependent structure. In case of firmwide incentives we find a similar pattern like in the self-contained interaction structure for both reward structures: The levels of performance achieved are rather independent from the intensities of the recency effect and from the anchoring effect. If departmental incentives are given in a full-interdependent interaction structure matters change with respect to the recency effect. Apparently, here the recency effect enfolds a productive effect: For all levels of the anchoring effect, the organizational performance increases with a more intense recency effect.

However, an interesting question is why the constellation of full-interdependent interactions combined with departmental incentives appears to be particularly sensitive to the recency effect. We argue that in this situation the reward structure generates an inadequate myopia: The incentive system lets the department heads focus only on the departmental performance of their choices while the choices also might have (negative or positive) cross-departmental effects. Thus, the organization likely is to suffer from a lower speed of performance enhancements as opportunities are missed (i.e., positive external effects are ignored) and

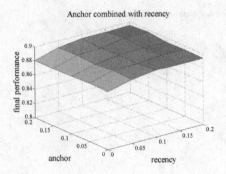

Fig. 11. Anchor & recency, full-interdep., departmental incentives

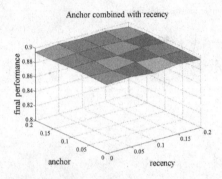

Fig. 12. Anchor & recency, full-interdep., firmwide incentives

bad alternatives are choosen (i.e., negative external effects are ignored). In this situation the recency effect induces more diversity in the search process and, by that, apparently increases final performance achieved.

4   Conclusion

The results suggest that, contrary to intuition, human decision-making biases do not necessarily reduce the overall performance achieved in collaborative decision-making processes. Instead, we found that in some constellations decision-making biases enfold beneficial effects. Of course, this puts claims for decision-making as rational as possible into perspective. Furthermore, our simulations reveal that decision-making biases partially compensate each other. The recency effect appears to compensate the status quo bias. With regard to the adaptive search processes this result might be explained as follows. The status quo bias on its own obviously even aggravates the well-known problem of adaptive search processes to stick to the local maximum in the performance landscape and, by that, to lead to inertia. In contrary, the recency effect has the potential to generate diversity in the search process in that eventually the status quo might be under-valued compared to a newly found alternative. These considerations indicate that the "right" combination of decision-making biases is of crucial relevance. However, we also found that organizational characteristics like the incentive system or the interaction structure among decisions might affect the effects of the decision-making biases in an organization.

Hence, the findings show that it might be a promising approach to analyze more into detail how the sequence of information provided to managers affects decision-making. Another issue relates to the underlying model structure: The NK model which serves as basis for our results involves certain assumptions, e.g., about the nature of the decision problem (binary decision problem) and performance contributions (drawn from a uniform distribution) which, of course, do not hold universally. These limitations as induced by the simulation approach chosen could be overcome in further research. Moreover, a combination with experimental research to the simulation method might be a further interesting approach. Furthermore, our model encapsulates three selected decision-making biases. Beyond these, for example, framing effects could be integrated in order to analyze the effect of the representation of information on decision-making in combination with other decision-making biases.

References

[1] Simon, H.A.: A behavioral model of rational choice. Quarterly Journal of Economics 69, 99–118 (1955)

[2] Bredenkamp, J., Wippich, W.: Lern- und Gedächtnispsychologie I. Kohlhammer W. (1989)

[3] Samuelson, W., Zeckhauser, R.: Status quo bias in decision making. Journal of Risk and Uncertainty 1(1), 7–59 (1988)

[4] Tversky, A., Kahneman, D.: Judgment under uncertainty: Heuristics and biases. Science 185(4157), 1124 (1974)

[5] Kahneman, D., Tversky, A.: The framing of decisions and the psychology of choice. Science, New Series 211(4481), 453–458 (1981)

[6] Bonabeau, E.: Agent-based modeling: methods and techniques for simulating human systems. Proceedings of the National Academy of Sciences of the United States of America 99(suppl. 3), 7280–7287 (2002)

[7] Moss, S.: Editorial introduction: Messy systems - the target for multi agent based simulation. In: Moss, S., Davidsson, P. (eds.) MABS 2000. LNCS (LNAI), vol. 1979, pp. 1–14. Springer, Heidelberg (2001)

[8] Van Dyke Parunak, H., Savit, R., Riolo, R.L.: Agent-based modeling vs. Equation-based modeling: A case study and users' guide. In: Sichman, J.S., Conte, R., Gilbert, N. (eds.) MABS 1998. LNCS (LNAI), vol. 1534, pp. 10–25. Springer, Heidelberg (1998)

[9] Kauffman, S.: The origins of order: Self-Organization and Selection in Evolution, vol. 209. Oxford University Press, New York (1993)

[10] Kauffman, S., Levin, S.: Towards a general theory of adaptive walks on rugged landscapes. Journal of Theoretical Biology 128(1), 11–45 (1987)

[11] Rivkin, J., Siggelkow, N.: Balancing search and stability: Interdependencies among elements organizational design. Management Science, 290–311 (2003)

[12] Siggelkow, N., Levinthal, D.: Temporarily divide to conquer: Centralized, decentralized, and reintegrated organizational approaches to exploration and adaptation. Organization Science, 650–669 (2003)

[13] Siggelkow, N., Rivkin, J.: Speed and search: Designing organizations for turbulence and complexity. Organization Science, 101–122 (2005)

[14] Chang, M.-H., Harrington, J.E.: Agent-Based Models of Organizations. Handbook of Computational Economics: Agent-Based Computational Economics, vol. 2, ch. 26, pp. 1273–1337. Elsevier (2006)

[15] Wall, F.: The (beneficial) role of informational imperfections in enhancing organisational performance. In: LiCalzi, M., Milone, L., Pellizzari, P. (eds.) Progress in Artificial Economics: Computational and Agent-Based Models. Lecture Notes in Economics and Mathematical Systems, vol. 645. Springer (2010)

[16] Kristensen, H., Gärling, T.: Anchoring induced biases in consumer price negotiations. Journal of Consumer Policy 23(4), 445–460 (2000)

[17] Kant, J.D., Thiriot, S.: Modeling one human decision maker with a multiagent system: the codage approach. In: Proceedings of the Fifth International Joint Conference on Autonomous Agents and Multiagent Systems, AAMAS 2006, pp. 50–57. ACM, New York (2006)

[18] An, L.: Modeling human decisions in coupled human and natural systems: Review of agent-based models. Ecological Modelling (2011)

[19] Masatlioglu, Y., Ok, E.: Rational choice with status quo bias. Journal of Economic Theory 121(1), 1–29 (2005)

Swarming Estimation of Realistic Mental Models

H. Van Dyke Parunak[1], Sven Brueckner[1], Elizabeth A. Downs[2], and Laura Sappelsa[3]

[1] Soar Technology, 3600 Green Court, Suite 600,
Ann Arbor, MI 48105 USA
[2] Jacobs Technology, 3520 Green Court, Suite 250,
Ann Arbor, MI 48105 USA
[3] Analytic Services, Inc., 2900 South Quincy Street,
Suite 800, Arlington, VA 22206
{van.parunak,sven.brueckner}@soartech.com,
liz.downs@jacobs.com, laura.sappelsa@anser.org

Abstract. Researchers have explored many formalisms to model how people think about their world. We describe an application that requires modeling how people forecast events in the real world. The naïve assumption is that they use formalisms that model how the world actually evolves. These formalisms are at variance with empirical psychological results. We present a more realistic alternative, the Narrative Space Model (NSM), describe a swarming agent algorithm to fit its parameters from observed data, and present some early results.

Keywords: Mental models, cognition, formal reasoning, narrative space model.

1   Introduction

In much agent research, software agents represent people, and the agent's internal code is based on a model of how people think. Some models, such as threshold-based decision rules (common in studies of opinion dynamics) and stochastic choices fitted to empirical data [25], make no claims to cognitive realism, though the former can be grounded in decision field theory [2]. Others, including utility maximization [12] and stochastic learning automata [16], assume that humans routinely apply axiomatically grounded theories to their daily decisions. Simon's "bounded rationality" [17] tempers this claim by observing that people do not have the processing power required to find true optima, but systems that invoke this approach (e.g., [5]) typically modify the amount of data to which they apply classical reasoning (such as utility maximization), and not the reasoning mechanisms themselves.

Our application, aggregation of forecasts from multiple experts, requires modeling how people form individual judgments. "Obvious" models of cognition are not adequate. We have devised an alternative, the Narrative Space Model (NSM), that other researchers may find useful. We show how swarming agents can fit a narrative space (NS) to observed data. The NSM may also be useful as a more realistic framework for agents intended to model human cognition.

F. Giardini and F. Amblard (Eds.): MABS 2012, LNAI 7838, pp. 43–55, 2013.
© Springer-Verlag Berlin Heidelberg 2013

Section 1 introduces our application. Section 2 summarizes the obvious candidates for modeling agents' cognition, and Section 3 summarizes research that shows their inadequacy. Section 4 describes the NSM. Section 5 tells how we fit it to observed data, and Section 6 discusses some fitted examples. Section 7 concludes.

2   Model-Based Forecast Aggregation

In many domains (e.g., intelligence analysis, business planning, and economic forecasting), human judgments are the most accessible, and sometimes the only, data on which to base decisions. The opinions of many people are often more accurate than those of a few [20]. One theory explaining this observation is that different people have different mental models of the domain, and the weight assigned to a given judgment in the aggregation should reflect how complementary its underlying model is to the models underlying other judgments [13].

To use this insight in aggregating forecasts, we must estimate forecasters' internal models from their forecasts. For example, "Will Bashar al-Assad remain President of Syria through 31 January 2012? (Yes/No)" A forecast consists of assigning a number to each possible response, such that the larger number corresponds to the outcome that the forecaster deems more likely, and the difference between the numbers reflects the forecaster's certainty in that estimate. Forecasters can update their forecasts over time. Table 1 summarizes a series of forecasts against this question from one forecaster. We wish to estimate the internal model that generates such data.

We assume a structural *Ansatz* that could generate numerical forecasts, then fit the *Ansatz* to the data. At first, we assumed that a mental model should look like a formal model of how the world evolves, perhaps with fewer variables to reflect bounded rationality. We considered a number of forms that deal in turn with *state variables*, *states*, and *statements* about the world.

We describe the state of the world by a vector of *state variables* $v = \{v_0 = t, v_1, ..., v_n\}$. In some cases, we want to remove time from the concept of state, and then we work with $u = v\backslash\{v_0\}$. For now we assume that this vector is of finite length and its elements are non-negative real numbers (for which we use the siglum $\Re$), though our framework generalizes naturally. The state of the world $s(t)$ is an element of $\Re^{n+1}$.

There are at least four traditional mathematical approaches to reasoning over such a system. Each has a distinctive representation, inference mechanism, and semantics.

A differential equation expresses the rate of change of *state variables* as a function of

Table 1. Example forecasts

Date	Forecast [1]
2011-11-10	{0.35,0.65}
2011-12-02	{0.3,0.7}
2011-12-19	{0.3,0.7}
2011-12-28	{0.4,0.6}
2012-01-04	{0.45,0.55}
2012-01-08	{0.6,0.4}
2012-01-11	{0.65,0.35}
2012-01-16	{0.7,0.3}
2012-01-17	{0.75,0.25}
2012-01-23	{0.8,0.2}
2012-01-29	{0.85,0.15}
2012-01-30	{0.95,0.05}

the current value of the state vector. Inference is by integration over time, which recovers the value of the state variables as a function of time. Differential equations (and difference equations for discrete time) are the most natural way to model a physical process, and they incorporate time as a first-class concept that can be quantified by how rapidly variables converge. In modeling social, political, and economic systems, differential equations are usually represented graphically by feedback diagrams such as those prominent in system dynamics [18].

Markov models manipulate, not state *variables*, but world *states*. To make this approach more tractable, the v_i are sometimes restricted to finite domains (for example, by binning the underlying values in $\Re^+$). Given a finite set of state variables, this binning yields a finite number of mutually exclusive, collectively exhaustive (MECE) world states. A discrete time, finite state Markov process[1] operates on a vector N ("now") indicating the probability that the world is in each possible state, by way of a matrix M whose elements express the probability that at the next time step the world will transition from the state indexed by the row to the state indexed by the column. Thus each row sums to 1. The matrix product $M \times N$ yields a new vector of state probabilities S'. This formalism requires MECE states: the system is in only one state at a time, and it is meaningless to talk about conditional probabilities between states.[2] A Markov process is a natural way to capture a causal semantics.

To avoid the Markovian explosion of states, we can deal with *statements* λ_i about the world rather than *states* of the world. A statement is a mapping from the power set of v to {True, False} (or to a degree of belief). A statement is true of all states of the world in which its variables match.[3] Thus this representation is the coarsest of the three that we have considered: statements represent sets of states, while states represent sets of assignments to variables. Because each statement can apply to multiple states of the world, we have no guarantee of statistical independence. In principle we must reason about the joint distribution of all statements, but domain-specific conditional constraints remove many conditioning links. Two traditional reasoning formalisms exploit such constraints, in different ways.

Formal logics deal with entailment relations among statements. They can handle only very limited subsets of 2^v, specifically those that support such relations. The inference mechanism is theorem proving.

Statements are objects of belief, and so are naturally manipulated by Bayesian mechanisms. Bayesian approaches capture domain constraints among statements graphically, either in a directed graph (a "Bayesian belief network," where each node records the probability of a statement conditioned on the probabilities of its parent statements) or an undirected graph (a Markov random field, where conditionality

---

[1] If the state space is defined over u instead of v, the Markov process is reversible.

[2] There are two caveats to this statement.

    1.   Bayesian approaches view the time series of statements *synchronically*, and define conditional probabilities over the sequence, working with v rather than u. In this case, superscripting the Markov step, the conditional probability $p(s^{i+1}|s^i)$ is just the Markov transition probability $p_{i,\,i+1}$. Reversible chains require more complicated approaches [3]. The mathematics can be aligned, but the semantics of conditional probability are quite different from those of transition probabilities.

    2.   The restriction to single states is classical; a quantum model could consider coexisting states in an evolving but unobserved system [22], a possibility we defer for now.

[3] More complex calculi than subsetting over v_i are possible. We retain the simpler representation of statements for expository clarity.

constraints are represented by adjacency and graph connectedness). The corresponding inference mechanism consists of various techniques for fitting the conditional probability tables that describe the relationship among linked statements. Logical reasoning is a reduced case of such reasoning [23], in which the nature of the statements permits particularly constrained conditional probability tables.

3   What People Do Not Do

Scientists and engineers model the world in terms of these mathematical structures, and naturally assume that people use some version of one or another of them in reasoning subjectively about how the world will evolve. In fact, the Bayesian formalism has long been characterized as "subjective probability" [9], because it defines probability in terms of "degree of belief." In spite of this characterization, there is persuasive evidence that most people do not manipulate their degrees of belief following Bayesian principles, or any of the other formalisms that we have discussed. We do not claim that people do not know how to perform the computations required in each of these formalisms, but simply observe that they do not do so in making routine judgments, even if they know how to do so with pencil and paper.

An important empirical challenge to structuring mental models as sets of differential equations (or the related difference equations or system dynamics models) is evidence that people do not reason effectively about feedback loops, that is, systems in which current values of variables affect future values of those same variables. The parade example of this failure is the beer game [19], a role-playing exercise involving a supply chain linking the production of a commodity (cases of beer in the canonical example) to consumers through a chain of distributors. Each link in the chain is represented by a human decision-maker, who receives orders from her customer (the adjacent link closer to the consumer) and formulates orders to her supplier (the adjacent link closer to the manufacturer). Players are rewarded for having sufficient inventory to respond to orders, and penalized for carrying excess inventory. All data in the system is visible to all the participants, and a simple set of difference equations would allow players to optimize their orders. But in fact, players regularly overrespond to changes in the level of demand, swinging between zero inventories that cost them sales and excess stocks that cost them a carrying charge. People do not use differential or difference equations to reason about how the world will change.

Human reasoning does have parallels to the inferencing process involved in Markov process models. Research on the "simulation heuristic" suggests that people think in terms of a series of putatively causal links in estimating the likelihood of a future event [11]: "Well, given where we are now, event A could make X true, which would allow B to happen, making Y true, and enabling C, which would result in the event we're considering." But these transitions are between *statements* about the world, not between mutually exclusive, collectively exhaustive (MECE) *states* of the world. A statement is a hyperplane through state space, asserting values for some state variables but leaving others unspecified. If the unspecified variables have multiple values, one can recover many states consistent with a single statement, violating the MECE condition. In addition, one can generate many related statements at different levels of specificity by leaving more and more variables undefined. For example, "al-Assad is assassinated," "al-Assad is dead," and "al-Assad is no longer president of Syria" are all different statements, but describe intersecting regions of state space. As a result, the independence axioms that permit calculations over transition probabilities in a Markov process are not admissible. Without such axioms, one cannot invoke the sum or product rules of conventional probability to interpret the numbers that people associate with individual transitions, or with the likelihood of a final outcome.

People also do not generally reach judgments through rigorous logical analysis. They can simultaneously hold mutually contradictory beliefs (such as whether Osama bin Laden is alive or dead), if those beliefs are related to a common underlying concept (i.e., that officials are involved in a cover-up) [24]. Further evidence is found in the logically sloppy nature of natural language. In English, people regularly interpret the conditional conjunction "if" as though it were equivalent to "if and only if."

Humans don't integrate differential equations, iterate Markov processes, or prove theorems when they forecast events. The probabilistic calculus that underlies a Bayesian system fares no better. Extensive studies [10] demonstrate that they routinely violate standard, rudimentary rules of probability. For example: people don't recognize

- that $P(A,B) \leq P(A)$, especially given a persuasive story that focuses attention on factors relevant to B;
- that if $P(A|B) > P(A|{\sim}B)$, then $P(B|A) > P(B|{\sim}A)$.
- that the variance of a sample decreases as the size of the sample increases;
- that if A causes B, then B is diagnostic of A;
- that base rate rate information should impact probability estimates;
- that dependence among probabilities matters. Even while commenting on people's weakness in probabilistic reasoning, Heuer [8] (pp. 156-157) advocates simply multiplying the probabilities of different characteristics of a scenario to get the probability of the overall scenario, without considering that those characteristics may be causally linked.

Remarkably, these effects persist even among experimental subjects with extensive expertise in formal methods [10]! Apparently, the formal methods are overwhelmed by strong, innate mechanisms of the human psyche. People can learn to manipulate formal methods in conscious "paper and pencil" reasoning, but their intuitive responses are usually very different from the formal methods that they have learned. Psychologists disagree about the reason for quantitative shortcomings [7], but the fact remains that probabilistic reasoning is a poor model of human cognition.

If one is building an agent to solve some problem (e.g., optimize a factory, or maximize profit in an on-line auction), these algorithms are excellent choices. But if one is constructing an agent to model what a person might do, these algorithms will be inaccurate. Whether these inaccuracies lead to problems in system-level behavior is an open question: in highly-constrained environments, system-level effects may be relatively independent of agent decision rules [15]. But a responsible modeler will be aware of the fiction involved in assuming that her agents are (for example) optimizing their utilities or computing beliefs based on conditional probabilities.

4   The Narrative Space Model

The psychological literature shows that people apply a number of heuristics in reasoning under uncertainty. In forecasting what will happen, they tend to think causally, rather than statistically [21], a tendency that would suggest an underlying model with a strong temporal component, such as differential equations and Markov processes as opposed to logic or conditional probabilities. However, experiments [11] show that people do not follow either of these models completely. The "atoms" that they assemble into temporal sequences are neither the changing values of *state variables* (as in a differential equation) nor MECE *states* (as in a Markov model). Instead, they are *statements* about the world, as in a Bayesian analysis. But the analysis is not Bayesian. Humans do not manipulate conditional probabilities, but cling to temporal sequencing. The dominant calculus in human reasoning appears to be the narrative, a sequence of statements about the world [6].

This hypothesis suggests that we express forecasters' mental models in terms of a space of possible narratives: statements (as in a logical or Bayesian representation) with transition weights between them (as in a Markov model) (Fig. 1).

- Dashed and dotted circles indicate statements that imply alternative outcomes to the forecasting question. For example, statements f and i might imply a "yes" answer to the al-Assad question, while statements h and j might imply a "no" answer.
- Dashed lines indicate inhibitory links: if one narrative trajectory has produced the node at the tail of a dashed arrow (e.g., b), it is less likely that the same user will also entertain a trajectory containing the node at the head of the arrow (in this case, e).
- The weight of the transition between two statements indicates how likely a given modeler is to move from the first to the second in her narrative. Fig. 1 does not represent these weights.

We call this graph (without weights on the edges) a "narrative space." Any trajectory through this space corresponds to a narrative that a user with the associated model could entertain. When we furnish a narrative space with transition probabilities, it becomes a "narrative generator," since we can sample it to generate a wide range of narratives.

An "outcome" in such a system is also a statement. Such a statement may appear as a node in the narrative generator. However, it may also be implied by other nodes. For example, if an outcome consists of $\{v_1 = 0, v_2 = 0\}$, this outcome is

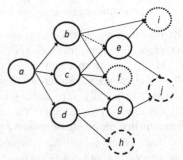

Fig. 1. A Narrative Space

implied by any statement that includes these assignments. Thus, in general, there is no single "outcome" node, but rather a set of nodes that imply various outcomes, as suggested by the dashed and dotted noted in Fig. 1.

Experiments show that the structure of a narrative carries more impact in subjective probability assessments than do formal probabilistic computations [4]. Given a narrative generator, some outcomes have few supporting narratives, and the transitions in these narratives are weak, yielding a low score. Conversely, if a statement implying an outcome is reachable by many alternative narratives, or narratives with strong transitions, the forecaster will tend to assign it a high score. The number that a forecaster assigns to an outcome is not an estimate of its probability in the real world, such as might be produced by one of the mathematical paradigms we reviewed, but rather a weighted count of the number of narratives generated by the forecaster's narrative generator that are compatible with the designated outcome.

To use a narrative generator to make forecasts, we sample trajectories from a designated "start" node to statements that imply outcomes. Repeated sampling leads to different outcomes. The numbers that a forecaster assigns to different outcomes are the proportion of samples that reach statements implying each outcome.

Fig. 2 is an example narrative space (NS), an abbreviation of a fuller model constructed by an experienced political analyst for the al-Assad question. The shaded node toward the top left is the start node, the shaded node at the upper right is an outcome node corresponding to a "no" answer, and the shaded node at the lower right is an outcome node for "yes." In addition, there is a default edge (not drawn) from every internal node to the lower-right outcome node, reflecting the possibility that the "no" node has not been reached when the problem expires. The question marks on the edges are place-holders for the transition weights that we fit as described in Section 5. Our fitting software takes as input an XML representation of the NS and a series of forecasts by a given forecaster, and replaces the "????" elements with transition weights.

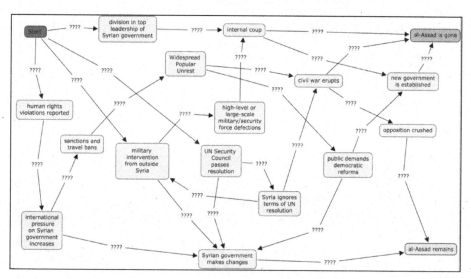

Fig. 2. Example Narrative Space (abbreviated)

Each node in Fig. 2 is a statement, and an arrow from one statement to another indicates that a trajectory following the arrow is a segment of a reasonable narrative. For example, the trajectory across the top of the figure generates the following narrative: "There is a division in the top leadership of the Syrian government. An internal coup takes place, removing al-Assad."

Fig. 2 is greatly abbreviated. The actual NS for this problem (Fig. 3) has 59 internal nodes and seven outcome nodes describing different ways that al-Assad might be removed. The labels reflect what is in the mind of the analyst who generates the graph, but how do we know where a forecaster is in this graph? There are three clues.

1. We maintain a log of news events that are relevant to each forecasting question, indexed to the node in the network that they attest. For example, one node in the full NS is labeled "Arab league refers crisis to UN," and on 24 January 2012, our log identified a news item stating that this had happened. As outlined in the next section, we use these news items to weight the fitting of transition probabilities to specific trajectories. News items provide a semantic link between forecasters and the graph, since we link news items to the graph and forecasters can adjust their forecasts based on news items.

2. Apart from the labels on nodes, the topology of transitions and inhibitory links gives the space an overall structure that favors certain narratives. Of the 182 transitions in Fig. 3, 59 (one for each internal node) go to "Yes" and are not drawn in the graph. If we apply our fitting process (Section 6) to a uniform forecast (0.5 yes, 0.5 no), paying no attention to news items, 49 of the transitions to "Yes" and 31 of the other transitions receive a probability of less than 0.1, pruning the graph by 44%. The reduced graph shows a limited set of story

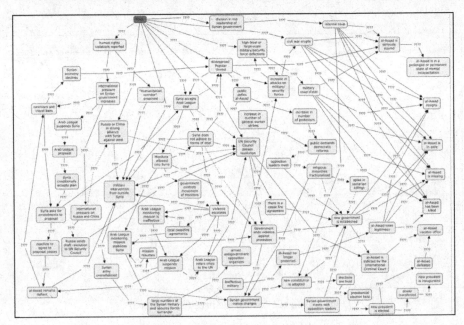

Fig. 3. Full Narrative Space for al-Assad question

beginnings and story endings, reflecting the default mental model of the expert who constructed the original graph. However, in the presence of evidence, some transitions that drop out of this "neutral" graph return, as we will illustrate in Section 7.

3. Our application requires distinguishing forecasters based on their underlying mental models, not deriving an exact representation of each model. Any model whose structure reflects the underlying narrative space, on which events can be localized, and that transforms forecasts into a signal characterizing the forecaster, serves our purpose. The NSM satisfies these requirements.

5   Probability Estimation in Narrative Spaces (PENS)

We characterize a given forecast by a set of transition weights in the NS that generates it. This set of weights is the forecast's "spectrum." Our algorithm for probability estimation in narrative spaces (PENS) is based on swarming agents.

PENS begins by starting at each outcome node and recursively marking all incoming links with the outcome states accessible along it.

For each question q and forecaster u, we have a series of forecasts $\hat{\theta}^{[q,t,u]}$ issued at times t. Each forecast in $\hat{\theta}^{[q,t,u]}$ is a tuple that assigns a probability to each outcome. We use the polyagent construct [14] to generate a set of edge weights γ_{ij} in the following way. For clarity, we restrict the discussion to forecasts made by a single user.

Each forecast is represented by a separate avatar agent at the start node that issues ghost agents for each outcome at a rate proportional to the forecast for that outcome. These ghosts move through the graph selecting randomly among the outgoing edges from each node that are labeled with their destination. Each ghost lays down pheromone tagged with the forecast time to mark the trajectory it is exploring, which corresponds to a possible narrative. Let $\Gamma^{[q,t,u]}$ be the set of transition probabilities γ_{ij} proportional to the final pheromone strengths on each link, generated from $\hat{\theta}^{[q,t,u]}$. By construction, if ghosts without a preference for outcome move through the graph from *Start* and choose transitions according to $\Gamma^{[q,t,u]}$, they will arrive at the outcome nodes in the proportions specified by $\hat{\theta}^{[q,t,u]}$.

At each node, a ghost chooses among outgoing edges that lead to its designated outcome, based on a roulette wheel over the value of a weighting function

$$Min(0, w_1 + w_2 \sum_{t' \leq t} \varphi^{t'} + w_3 \sum_{t' \leq t} \varepsilon^{t'} - w_4 \alpha^{t'}) \tag{1}$$

- $\varphi^{t'}$ is the pheromone deposited by previous ghosts from an avatar representing a forecast made at time t'. Each ghost attends to ghost pheromone from its own and all earlier avatars. Earlier avatars represent earlier forecasts by the same user on the same question, favoring generators that differ as little as possible from earlier ones.

- $\varepsilon^{t'}$ is event pheromone from a node that has been confirmed by a news event.

- $\alpha^{t'}$ is inhibitory pheromone resulting from inhibitory links terminating at the destination node, and heuristically, its weight w_4 can be set equal to the weight w_2 of the ghost pheromone.
- w_1 provides for equal choice among links in the case where there is no pheromone in place; its magnitude relative to the other weights determines the degree to which ghosts respond to pheromones (favored by small w_1) vs. simply following the structure of the graph (favored by large w_1)

Ghosts from a forecaster's first forecast favor destination statements that are marked as having occurred, but otherwise choose uniformly among eligible outgoing edges. As a forecaster makes subsequent forecasts, ghosts from those forecasts weight their choices of outgoing edges based on pheromone from ghosts of previous forecasts, and also take into account nodes marked by more recent news reports.

6   Examples

We consider three narrative generators that result from applying the PENS algorithm to Fig. 3. First, we fit a neutral forecast (50% assigned to each outcome), in the absence of any event information (w_3 in (1) set to 0, other weights to 1). Then we turn on event information, and fit the first forecast in Table 1, then all the forecasts in that table. In all cases, we delete edges with a weight < 0.1.

Fitting a homogeneous forecast with no event information reveals the "natural" topology of the graph, taking into account divergent and convergent paths and the effect of inhibitory links. The NS identifies nine possible starting statements for a narrative about al-Assad's fall. The intrinsic topology of the space favors only five of these, but with roughly equal probabilities. In addition, of the seven possible outcome nodes representing al-Assad's removal, two (exile and death) are not reachable in this neutral generator. The most likely narrative is that civil war erupts, leading to al-Assad's being seriously injured, but not sidelined by the time the deadline arrives.

An interesting difference between the neutral generator and the NS concerns a node in the NS representing the statement, "Government ends violence against protestors." Fig. 4 shows a fragment of Fig. 3 that involves this statement. The statement is part of several narratives in which it is preceded by UN action or an Arab league monitoring mission, and leads either to changes in the existing Syrian government or to a new government. Of particular interest is the inhibitory link between "Syria does not adhere to terms of deal" and "Government ends violence ...." The focal statement is part of a credible narrative only in a world in which diplomatic activities are prominent and Syria is going along with them.

The generator from a homogeneous forecast with no events does not include this node. Multiple paths lead from Start rather directly to "Syria accepts Arab league deal," but also to "Syria does not adhere to terms of deal," and the inhibitory link represses transitions to "Government ends violence ...."

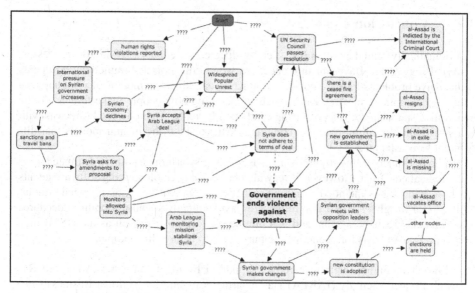

Fig. 4. Narrative neighborhood of "Government ends violence…"

The generator from the entire series of forecasts in Table 1, with event weighting turned on, also does not include "Government ends violence …." This generator supports only narratives starting with "human rights violations," followed most strongly by "International pressure on Syrian government increases." These two nodes are the second and third most highly attested in the log of news events, at 68 and 59 out of 421 events. (The node most often attested in the news, "al-Assad remains defiant" at 70 references, is buried deeply in the graph, but does form part of this generator.) Though the generator supports trajectories including diplomatic efforts, the fourth most attested statement (55 events) is "Syria does not adhere to terms of deal," strongly activating the inhibitory link and repressing "Government ends violence…."

However, the generator fit to the first forecast in Table 1 *does* support narratives that include "Government ends violence …." At the time of the first forecast (10 Nov 2011), only three nodes in the NS had associated events in the event log: "human rights violations reported," "international pressure on syrian government increases," and "sanctions and travel bans." All three events reinforce narratives beginning with human rights violations, so this generator, like the generator from all of Table 1, supports only narratives that start in this way (suppressing the other four starting statements from the uniform forecast). However, at this time no events attest "Syria does not adhere to terms of deal," so "Government ends violence" remains active.

Thus the PENS algorithm is able to distinguish the intrinsic non-uniform topology of a NS, and generate distinct spectra that are a function of the forecast itself, the history of previous forecasts by a given forecaster, and known events that occurred during the forecast period. These spectra enable us to characterize the uniformity or diversity of the underlying models held by each of our forecasters.

7   Conclusion

Axiomatically sound procedures, such as differential equations, Markov processes, formal logics, and Bayesian inference, are wonderful tools for implementing agents that solve problems for us. They are completely unrealistic as models of what happens in peoples' minds. In some cases (such as modeling how people make forecasts), the narrative space model is a promising candidate. It can be fit to observed forecasts with a swarming algorithm, characterizing and distinguishing the mental models that different forecasters use.

The relevance of this study to agents is in using swarming agents to estimate a psychological construct. However, it may also be useful in implementing software agents whose behavior is intended to mimic realistic human reasoning, as in social simulations. Our insights suggest that reliance on axiomatically sound reasoning procedures will yield unrealistic agents, and that alternative formalisms (such as the NSM) may be a preferable basis for agents whose purpose is to behave like people.

Acknowledgements. This research is supported by the Intelligence Advanced Research Projects Activity (IARPA) via Department of Interior National Business Center contract number D11PC20060. The U.S. Government is authorized to reproduce and distribute reprints for Governmental purposes notwithstanding any copyright annotation thereon. Disclaimer: The views and conclusions contained herein are those of the authors and should not be interpreted as necessarily representing the official policies or endorsements, either expressed or implied, of IARPA, DoI/NBC, or the U.S. Government.

References

[1] Arulampalam, S., Maskell, S., Gordon, N., Clapp, T.: A Tutorial on Particle Filters for On-line Non-linear/Non-Gaussian Bayesian Tracking. IEEE Transactions on Signal Processing 50, 174–188 (2001)

[2] Busemeyer, J.R., Townsend, J.T.: Decision Field Theory: A Dynamic-Cognitive Approach to Decision Making in an Uncertain Environment. Psychological Review 100(3), 432–459 (1993)

[3] Diaconis, P., Rolles, S.W.W.: Bayesian analysis for reversible Markov chains. Ann. Statist. 34(3), 1270–1292 (2006)

[4] Dieckmann, N.F.: Communicating Risk in Intelligence Forecasts: The Consumer's Perspective. Thesis at University of Oregon, Department of Dept. of Psychology (2007)

[5] Filatova, T., Parker, D., van der Veen, A.: Agent-Based Urban Land Markets: Agent's Pricing Behavior, Land Prices and Urban Land Use Change. Journal of Artificial Societies and Social Simulation 12(1), 3 (2009)

[6] Fisher, W.R.: Human Communication as Narration: Toward a Philosophy of Reason, Value, and Action. University of South Carolina Press, Columbia (1989)

[7] Gigerenzer, G.: Bounded and Rational. In: Stainton, R.J. (ed.) Contemporary Debates in Cognitive Science, Contemporary Debates in Philosophy, vol. 7, pp. 115–133. Blackwell, Oxford (2006)

[8] Heuer Jr., R.J.: Psychology of Intelligence Analysis. Center for the study of intelligence, Central Intelligence Agency (1999)

[9]   Jeffrey, R.: Subjective Probability: The Real Thing. Cambridge University Press, Cambridge (2004)

[10] Kahneman, D., Slovic, P., Tversky, A. (eds.): Judgment under uncertainty: Heuristics and Biases. Cambridge Univ. Press, Cambridge (1982)

[11] Kahneman, D., Tversky, A.: The Simulation Heuristic. In: Kahneman, D., Slovic, P., Tversky, A. (eds.) Judgment Under Uncertainty: Heuristics and Biases, pp. 201–208. Cambridge University Press, Cambridge (1982)

[12] Millington, J., Romero-Calcerrada, R., Wainwright, J., Perry, G.: An Agent-Based Model of Mediterranean Agricultural Land-Use/Cover Change for Examining Wildfire Risk. Journal of Artificial Societies and Social Simulation 11(4) (2008)

[13] Page, S.E.: The Difference: How the Power of Diversity Creates Better Groups, Firms, Schools, and Societies. Princeton University Press, Princeton (2007)

[14] Van Dyke Parunak, H., Brueckner, S.: Concurrent Modeling of Alternative Worlds with Polyagents. In: Antunes, L., Takadama, K. (eds.) MABS 2006. LNCS (LNAI), vol. 4442, pp. 128–141. Springer, Heidelberg (2007)

[15] Van Dyke Parunak, H., Brueckner, S., Savit, R.: Universality in Multi-Agent Systems. In: Proceedings of Third International Joint Conference on Autonomous Agents and Multi-Agent Systems (AAMAS 2004), pp. 930–937. ACM (2004)

[16] Power, C.: A Spatial Agent-Based Model of N-Person Prisoner's Dilemma Cooperation in a Socio-Geographic Community. Journal of Artificial Societies and Social Simulation 12(1), 8 (2009)

[17] Simon, H.A.: The Sciences of the Artificial. MIT Press, Cambridge (1969)

[18] Sterman, J.: Business Dynamics. McGraw-Hill, New York (2000)

[19] Sterman, J.D.: Modeling Managerial Behavior: Misperceptions of Feedback in a Dynamic Decision Making Experiment. Management Science 35(3), 321–339 (1989)

[20] Surowiecki, J.: The Wisdom of Crowds: Why the Many are Smarter Than the Few and How Collective Wisdom Shapes Business, Economies, Societies and Nations. Doubleday, New York (2004)

[21] Tversky, A., Kahneman, D.: Causal schemas in judgments under uncertainty. In: Kahneman, D., Slovic, P., Tversky, A. (eds.) Judgment under Uncertainty: Heuristics and Biases, pp. 117–128. Cambridge University Press, Cambridge (1982)

[22] van Rijsbergen, C.J.: The Geometry of Information Retrieval. Cambridge University Press, Cambridge (2004)

[23] Williamson, J.: Combining probability and logic: introduction. Journal of Logic, Language and Information 15(1-2), 1–3 (2006)

[24] Wood, M.J., Douglas, K.M., Sutton, R.M.: Dead and Alive: Beliefs in Contradictory Conspiracy Theories. Social Psychological and Personality Science (2012) (forthcoming)

[25] Yang, C., Kurahashi, S., Kurahashi, K., Ono, I., Terano, T.: Agent-Based Simulation on Women's Role in a Family Line on Civil Service Examination in Chinese History. Journal of Artificial Societies and Social Simulation 12(2), 5 (2009)

Revisiting the El Farol Problem: A Cognitive Modeling Approach

Davi D'Andréa Baccan and Luis Macedo

University of Coimbra,
Centre for Informatics and Systems of the University of Coimbra,
Department of Informatics Engineering, Polo II, 3030, Coimbra, Portugal
{baccan,macedo}@dei.uc.pt

Abstract. Decentralized market economies are complex systems that involve large numbers of heterogeneous participants. A good abstraction of this scenario is illustrated by the El Farol problem. In this problem, there is a bar with a fixed capacity and a given number of participants need to choose between either stay at home or go to the bar. However, if the attendance is above or equals the capacity of the bar, it becomes too crowded and the participants who attended did not have fun. In this paper we provide insight into the behaviour of the participants in those decentralized market economies scenarios by using a cognitive modelling approach in the El Farol problem. In three computer experiments we investigate, compare, and discuss a number of features of our agent-based model namely the relationship between beliefs and strategies, emotions of cognitive agents, as well as other aspects of market dynamics.

1 Introduction

Traditional economic theories tend to assume that agents are rational in the sense that they form expectations rationally and are able to make optimal decisions [10]. In other words, agents are considered to be able to correctly form probabilistic assessments, calculating which of the alternative courses of action maximize their expected utility (e.g. [26, 6]). On the other hand, observations regarding the behaviour of agents in real life scenarios, together with behavioral economics [14] findings constitute evidence that agents are not fully rational (e.g. [17, 11]). Agents do not always have enough time or the cognitive ability to process all the related information with accuracy, that is to say that they have bounded rationality.

A good example of a scenario in which agents have bounded rationality and need to make decisions essentially based on inductive reasoning and, therefore, cognitive agents might be used is illustrated by the El Farol problem [1]. In this problem, there is a bar with a fixed capacity and a certain number of people need to periodically and independently choose between two actions, namely go the bar or stay at home. However, if the number of people who go the bar is above or equals its capacity the bar becomes too crowded and those who attended did not have fun. In this problem agents generally make use of a strategy that provides

F. Giardini and F. Amblard (Eds.): MABS 2012, LNAI 7838, pp. 56–68, 2013.

them with a forecast for the next attendance that ultimately indicates whether the best action is to stay at home or go the bar. The only information available is the historical attendance and there is no communication between agents. In the context of those scenarios, unlike traditional economic theories, agents are somewhat forced to be heterogeneous in the sense they have to employ, for instance, different strategies or mechanisms for creating predictions about the next attendance. Nevertheless, as a strategic environment, the result heavily depends on the choice made by other agents.

The El Farol problem offers a rich set of possibilities for investigation as well as an interesting dynamics with respect to the behaviour of agents both in terms of micro and macro perspectives. It is important to stress that the interest in the El Farol problem is not new. On the contrary, a variety of different approaches have been proposed (e.g. [5, 19, 20]). For instance, Cross et al. [9] tried to incorporate minimal psychological factors to the El Farol, and observe whether they are able to reproduce some statistical regularities that are often found in real market data across different markets and periods of time, known as stylized facts [7]. Interestingly, despite its simplicity, their model was able to simulate a small number of fundamental phenomena.

In this paper we employ a cognitive modeling approach to observe the behaviour of agents in the context of the El Farol problem. It means that artificial agents will be empowered with mechanisms similar to or inspired in those used by humans. Therefore, the behaviour of artificial agents tends to be closer to the behaviour of humans in a similar scenario. In three computer experiments we investigate, compare, and discuss a number of features of our agent-based model namely the relationship between beliefs and strategies, emotions of cognitive agents, as well as other aspects of market dynamics.

The paper is organized as follows. In Section 2 we briefly present the cognitive emotion theories concepts related to our work. In Section 3 we present our agent-based model. In Section 4 we detail the experimental setup of our computer experiments and show our results, while in Section 5 we discuss our results. Finally, in Section 6 we conclude the paper and point out some future directions.

2   Cognitive Emotion Theories

Cognitive emotion theories (e.g. [15, 27]) rely on the assumption that emotions are mental states elicited as a result of the evaluation or appraisal of stimuli of all kinds (e.g. actions, events) and can be computed in terms of cognitions (beliefs) and motives (desires). Beliefs are mental states in which one holds a particular proposition to be true, whereas desires represent the motives or future states that one wants to accomplish.

The Belief-Desire Theory of Emotions (BDTE) is a cognitive emotion theory consisted of propositions, beliefs, desires, new beliefs, and two hard-wired comparator mechanisms, namely the Belief-Belief Comparator (BBC) and the Belief-Desire Comparator (BDC) [27]. The conceptual framework of the BDTE is the same as the belief-desire theory of action which inspired the BDI (belief-desire-intention) approach to artificial agents [3].

A proposition p is represented as a tuple $\langle S, B, D \rangle$ where S is the mental language expressing the proposition p, B and D are quantities representing, respectively, the agent's degree of belief and desire regarding proposition p. The strength of a belief in a proposition p at time t, defined as $b(p,t)$, is a value $\in [0.0, 1.0]$, where 1.0 denotes certainty that p, 0.5 maximal uncertainty, and 0.0 certainty that not p. Similarly, the strength of a desire about a proposition p at time t, defined as $d(p,t)$, might be a value, for instance, $\in [-100, +100]$. Positive values denote desire in favor of p, negative values denote desire against p, and 0 denotes indifference. A new belief is the belief or fact in a proposition that agents receive basically through its sensors (e.g. vision and hearing in the case of a human agent). It is defined as a tuple $\langle S, B, * \rangle$, where $*$ denotes that the desire is irrelevant for new beliefs.

The Belief-Belief Comparator (BBC) compares each newly acquired belief to all pre-existing beliefs, looking for either a match or a mismatch. A match means that a pre-existing belief was confirmed by the newly acquired belief, whereas a mismatch means that a pre-existing belief was disconfirmed. As a result, BBC yields either a belief-confirmation signal or a belief-disconfirmation signal. Similarly, the Belief-Desire Comparator (BDC) compares each newly acquired belief to all pre-existing desires, looking for either a match or a mismatch. A match means that a desire was "fulfilled", whereas a mismatch means that a desire was "frustrated". As a result, BDC yields either a desire-fulfillment signal or a desire-frustration signal.

BDTE defines emotions as products or signals produced by the BBC and BDC. Additionally, defining whether agents experience non neutral emotions (e.g. happiness, unhappiness) depends on the desire of agents regarding p. An agent would be happy about p at time t, if she/he is currently certain that p happens, and has a desire in favor of p, i.e. $d(p,t) > 0$. On the other hand, surprise is elicited only based on beliefs. Formally, surprise can be defined as a peculiar state of mind, usually of brief duration, caused by unexpected events, or proximally the detection of a contradiction or conflict between newly acquired and pre-existing beliefs (e.g. [24, 22]). Therefore, an agent would experience surprise regarding p, if at time t_{-1} she/he had some belief that p will happen, but receives the new belief that actually non p happens. In Table 1 we summarize how the emotions we use in this work are computed from a qualitative perspective.

However, the BDTE does not clearly define how to compute surprise. Therefore, in the context of artificial surprise for artificial agents two models can be stressed namely the model proposed by Macedo and Cardoso [23, 21] and the model proposed by Lorini and Castelfranchi (e.g. [18]). Both models were mainly inspired by a cognitive-psychoevolutionary model of surprise proposed by Meyer et al. A detailed description of the similarities and differences of the models, written by Macedo, Cardoso, Reisenzein, Lorini, and Castelfranchi, can be found at [22]. The model proposed by Macedo and Cardoso offers a straightforward and easy way of computing artificial surprise that we consider to be the most appropriate for this work. Macedo and Cardoso claim that the relation between the subjective probability and the intensity of surprise about an

Table 1. Belief-desire theory of emotions, qualitative formulation (adapted from [27]). The notation is as follows: $Bel(p, t)$ stands for "believes p at time t", $Certain(p, t)$ stands for "firmly believes p at t", $Des(p, t)$ stands for "desires p at t", and $Des(\neg p, t)$ stands for "desires not-p at t, $\neg$ is aversive against p at t".

Emotion	if	Belief at t	Desire at t	Belief at t_{-1}
$happy(p, t)$		$Certain(p, t)$	$Des(p, t)$	
$unhappy(p, t)$		$Certain(p, t)$	$Des(\neg p, t)$	
$surprised(p, t)$		$Certain(p, t)$	(irrelevant)	$Bel(\neg p, t_{-1})$

event E_g from a set of mutually exclusive events $\{E_1, ..., E_n\}$ can be described by $Surprise(E_g) = log_2(1 + P(E_h) - P(E_g))$ where E_h is the event with the highest subjective probability in the set.

For calculating non neutral emotions we rely on the BDTE [27], whereas for calculating surprise we rely on the artificial surprise model proposed by Macedo and Cardoso [23]. Similar to Table 1, in Table 2 we summarize how the emotions we use in this work are computed from a qualitative perspective.

Table 2. Belief-desire theory of emotions, quantitative formulation (adapted from [27]). The $b(p, t)$ represents the strength of belief in p at time t, with 1 denoting certainty that p, 0.5 maximal uncertainty, and 0 certainty that not-p. $d(p, t)$ represents the direction and strength of the desire for p at time t, with values > 0 denoting positive desire, 0 indifference, and values < 0 aversion against p. $Happiness(p, t)$, $Unhappiness(p, t)$ are the emotion intensities, ranging from 0 (absence of the emotion) to some maximum number, in this work 100. Regarding the calculation of surprise, $P(E_h)$ is the highest subjective probability attributed to an event from a set of mutually exclusive events, and $P(E_g)$ is the subjective probability of the event that actually happened [23].

Emotion Intensity in function of d and b	for domain subset (else emotion intensity = 0)
$Happiness(p, t)$	$b(p, t) = 1$ & $d(p, t) > 0$
$Unhappiness(p, t)$	$b(p, t) = 1$ & $d(p, t) < 0$
$Surprise(p, t)$	$log_2(1 + P(E_h) - P(E_g))$

3 Agent-Based Model

We distinguish two main aspects related with our agent model we used: (i) empowering agents with the BDTE; and, (ii) providing the agents with ways for dealing with information, for representing preferences, and for learning and evolving. These aspects are described in more detail as follows.

Firstly, our model was developed in the JABM (Java Agent Based Modeling) [25] that is a powerful Java API for developing agent-based simulation models using a discrete-event simulation framework. Therefore, we empowered JABM artificial agents with the Belief-Desire Theory of Emotions (BDTE). It included the implementation of the underlying mechanisms for dealing with propositions, beliefs, desires, new beliefs, with the BBC and BDC comparators, and also with the model proposed by Macedo and Cardoso. Additionally, inspired in the highly sophisticated, complex and dynamic human memory mechanism (see [8, 2] for an extensive review), we empowered agents with two different memory systems namely short-term memory and long-term memory as well as with the processes of encoding, storing (including forgetting), and retrieving memories. Therefore, agents are able to deal with previous knowledge with respect to whether the current strategy succeeded or failed and use such knowledge to calculate its current belief in the strategy.

Secondly, in designing the artificial agents we addressed the following three main design questions (e.g. [16].

The first question is how artificial agents deal with information. Consistent with the classical El Farol problem definition [1], agents receive only endogenous information that is the only information available is the historical attendance.

The second question includes all issues related to how to represent the preferences of artificial agents. The first issue is the definition of not only which strategies will be available for agents to forecast the next attendance but also the specification of all parameters related to those strategies. Agents have available six strategies commonly used in the context of the El Farol problem, namely noise trader strategy (NT), simple moving average strategy (SMA), exponential moving average strategy (EMA), opposite strategy (OPS), same strategy (SAS), and lagged strategy (LAS). The NT generates a uniformly distributed forecast between 0 and 100. The SMA generates a forecast using a simple moving average with a given window size, uniformly chosen between 2 and 100. The EMA generates a forecast using a moving average with a given window size in which recent values referring to the attendance gain more weight as opposed to old values. The OPS generates a forecast that is the opposite of the last week, whereas the SAS generates a forecast that is the same of the last week. Last but not least, the LAS generates a forecast that is exactly the same as a given past week, uniformly chosen between 1 and 5. The second issue is the definition of whether agents will use a fixed strategy or if they will be allowed to change from the current strategy to a new strategy based on some criteria. Agents have available two different scenarios. In the first, agents use a fixed strategy (henceforth referred to as FS) that means that once the strategy is defined, before the beginning of the experiment, the artificial agent will use this strategy until the end. In the second, agents can change from the current strategy to a new strategy (henceforth referred to as CS) based on their belief regarding whether they believe the strategy works or not, as we will explain in details later in this section.

The third design question refers to how artificial agents learn from mistakes and evolve. For each round, one of the strategies mentioned earlier is used by agents to predict whether the bar will be crowded or not and therefore indicates to them if the best action is either to stay at home or go the bar. Therefore, a strategy succeeds when it indicates the correct action or, in other words, if the strategy predicted that the bar will be crowded (or not) and it turned out to be crowded (or not) the action indicated by the strategy was the correct (wrong) one. Therefore, when a strategy succeeds (fails) an agent increases (decreases) its belief in the correctness of the strategy, based on a Bayesian process. According to the BDTE, the previous scenario can be modelled as follows. S that is the mental language expressing the proposition p is defined as "My strategy works", and the strength of a belief in the proposition p at time t, defined as $b(p,t)$, is a value $\in [0.0, 1.0]$, where 1.0 denotes certainty that the strategy really works, 0.5 denotes maximal uncertainty that is the agent does not know whether the strategy works or not, and 0.0 denotes certainty that the strategy does not work. The $b(p,t)$ is calculated considering the experience of the agent in using the current strategy in a given number of last rounds, that is its memory size (henceforth referred to as MS). For example, suppose the unlikely scenario in which an agent is using a strategy that worked in the last 100 rounds. In this case, the $b(p,t)$ would be close to 1.0, meaning that the agent "firmly believes" its strategy works.

Practically, on the one hand, a $b(p,t) > 0.5$ means that the agent has some degree of belief in the fact that its current strategy works and so it makes sense to a "rational" agent to maintain using the current strategy. On the other hand, a $b(p,t) < 0.5$ means that the agent has some degree of belief in the fact that its current strategy does not work and so it makes sense changing to a new strategy. Finally, in the context of our experiments, if $b(p,t) == 0.5$ the agent maintain using the current strategy. In this context, for the CS scenario, we defined a belief threshold (henceforth referred to as BT) of 0.5 by which the agent must change its current strategy. Therefore, an agent only changes its current strategy if and only if $b(p,t) < 0.5$. Additionally, when an agent starts using a strategy its initial $b(p,t) = 0.5$.

It is also important to present some underlying concepts we employed, namely the concept of global belief in the strategy, global surprise, and cumulative happiness. Global belief in the strategy (henceforth referred to as GBS) is the sum of all $b(p,t)$ and that is the "global belief that the strategy works". Global surprise (henceforth referred to as GSu) is the sum of all surprise "felt" by agents that is the "global surprise felt by agents with respect to whether their strategy works or not". Cumulative happiness (henceforth referred to as CuH) is the cumulative sum of all happiness "felt" by agents. An agent "feel" happiness when its strategy works or, in other words, when it indicates the correct action. We assume all agents "firmly desire" the strategy to work that is to say, according to the BDTE, that each agent has a $d(p,t) = +100$. In Table 3 we summarize the acronyms used throughout the paper, describe its meanings, and explain how we compute each of them.

To illustrate how CuH, GBS, and GSu work, consider the following example. Assume that there are two groups of agents namely G1 and G2. G1 consists of 59 agents using a fixed strategy that indicates the action go to the bar, whereas G2 consists of 41 agents using a fixed strategy that indicates the action stay at home. In this context, the attendance would be 59 and therefore the right action to take would be go to the bar. Therefore, for each round all agents of G1 would "feel" happiness, while all agents of G2 agents would "feel" unhappiness. Practically, in the first round, $CuH = 590$, in the second round, $CuH = 1180$ *(590+590)* and so forth. It is worth noting that this is the scenario that provides optimal results in terms of CuH and that such optimal values are used by us as references for calculating and plotting the results of CuH throughout the paper. Additionally, the $b(p, t)$ of all agents of G1 would be close to 1.0, while the $b(p, t)$ of all agents of G2 agents would be close to 0.0. GBS in this example tends to its maximum possible value that is 59. Regarding GSu, for all agents the $surprise(p, t)$ would be 0.0 and consequently GSu would be also 0.0.

Table 3. Summary of the main acronyms, meanings, and its respective forms of calculation

Acronym	Meaning	Calculation
CuH	Cumulative happiness	Cumulative sum of all happiness (i.e. its strategy worked)
GBS	Global belief in the strategy	Sum of the individual $b(p, t)$ of all agents
GSu	Global surprise	Sum of the individual $surprise(p, t)$ "felt" by all agents

4 Experiments and Results

We conducted three computer experiments to explore how the cognitive agents we modelled behave in the context of the El Farol problem. In Table 4 we summarize the features of the experiments. The experiments are defined in terms of the Strategies, and Fixed Strategy (FS) or Changing Strategy (CS) scenario. For all experiments memory size (MS) is 100, $BT = 0.5$, initial $b(p,t) = 0.5$, $d(p, t) = +100$, number of rounds is 2000 and, consistent with the seminal paper on the El Farol [1], the number of agents is 100 and the capacity is of 60. Due to the nature of the experiments, we run E1 five times so that we have five different configurations concerning the distribution of the strategies. Conversely, we run E2 and E3 just one time.

In the context of the CS scenario, the basic algoritm for changing a strategy is as follows. At the start of the simulation, each agent needs to select a strategy. During the simulation, if and only if $b(p, t) < BT$ an agent needs to change its current strategy by selecting one of the remaining strategies. When an agent has tested all the strategies, he/she changes to the strategy selected at the start of the simulation, creating a cycle. All strategies have the same probability of being selected.

Table 4. Experiments are defined as follows: **Strategy(ies)**: noise trader strategy (NT), simple moving average strategy (SMA), exponential moving average strategy (EMA), opposite strategy (OPS), same strategy (SAS), and lagged strategy (LAS); and **FS/CS**: fixed strategy (FS) or changing strategy (CS) scenario. For all experiments, number of rounds is 2000, belief threshold (BT) is 0.5, initial belief in strategy ($b(p,t)$) = 0.5, $d(p, t) = +100$, capacity of the bar is 60, the number of agents is 100, and memory size (MS) is 100. We run E1 five times, E2 and E3 one time.

Exp.	Strategy(ies)	FS/CS
1	NT, SMA, EMA, OPS, SAS, LAS	FS
2	NT, SMA, EMA, OPS, SAS, LAS	CS
3	NT	FS

We show and compare the results of our experiments both over time and in general. All outliers were removed and in some situations we smoothed and magnified the data in order to make the presentation clearer and the understanding easier. Such modifications are clearly indicated in graphics, otherwise the data is in its original scale.

We first show in Figure 1 the results regarding the attendance. In Figure 2 we show the results regarding CuH (cumulative happiness). GBS (global belief in strategy) and GSu (global surprise) "felt" by agents are shown in Figures 3 and 4, respectively.

We can see in Figure 1 that the attendances of E1 are quite similar, while the attendance of E2 (red) resembles the attendance of E3 (green). Additionally, E1 exhibits more volatile attendances than E2 and E3. Regarding CuH (cumulative happiness), we can see in Figure 2 that E1 has values that are considerably lower

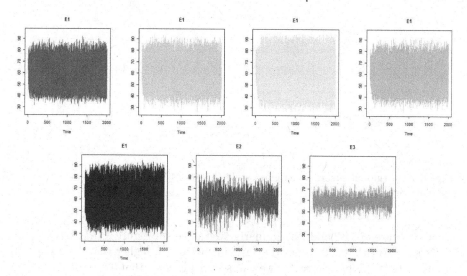

Fig. 1. Attendance of all experiments

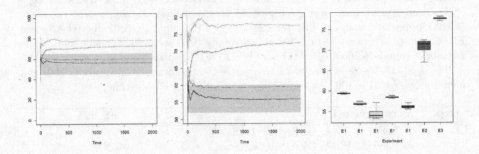

Fig. 2. *CuH* (cumulative happiness): original scale (left), zoomed in (center), boxplot (right). Gray area indicates runs of E1.

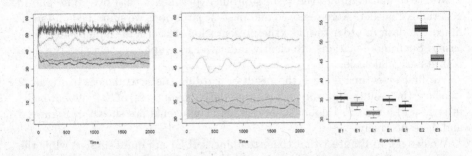

Fig. 3. *GBS* (global belief in strategy): zoomed in (left), SMA=100 and zoomed in (center), boxplot (right). Gray area indicates runs of E1.

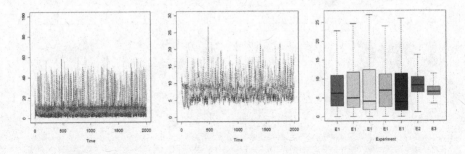

Fig. 4. *GSu* (global surprise): original scale (left), SMA=10 and zoomed in (center), boxplot (right)

when compared to E2 and E3. Similarly, we can see in Figure 3 that *GBS* values of E1 are lower than E2 values that are, in their turn, higher than E3 values. In terms of *GSu* (global surprise), we can see in Figure 4 that *GSu* oscillates in a narrow range between 0 and 30 for all experiments.

5   Discussion

In analyzing the results we were especially interested in observing the relationship•between beliefs and strategies that is the belief in strategies (GBS), emotions of cognitive agents namely happiness (CuH) and surprise (GSu), as well as other aspects of market dynamics.

First of all, we need to bear in mind that there is an inherent relationship between memory size (MS), belief in strategy ($b(p,t)$) and consequently the global belief in strategy (GBS), and global surprise (GSu). The memory size (MS) is used to store the experience in using the strategy, specifically whether the action indicated by the strategy proved to be right or wrong. Practically, the MS refers to a given number of last rounds which the agent is able to "remember", as we mentioned earlier in Section 3. Such knowledge is latter retrieved so that the belief in strategy ($b(p,t)$) can be calculated and consequently its global sum that is the global belief in strategy (GBS). Additionally, according to the artificial surprise model proposed by Macedo and Cardoso, surprise varies from 0.0 to 1.0 and the closer the $b(p,t)$ is to the point of maximal uncertainty, that means a belief in strategy ($b(p,t)$) equals 0.5, the lower is the individual surprise and consequently its global value (GSu).

From the results we can draw the following conclusions.

First, in all experiments, agents need to create a belief with respect to whether the current strategy works or not. Therefore there are only two mutually exclusive outcomes about the proposition. For instance, assume the outcome "strategy works" referred to as $O1$ and the outcome "strategy does not work" referred to as $O2$, and an agent that has a $b(p,t) = 0.7$ in $O1$ and therefore a complementary belief of 0.3 in $O2$. On the one hand, if the strategy succeeded, the surprise "felt" by the agent would be 0 ($Surprise(E_g) = log_2(1 + 0.70 - 0.70)$), according to the artificial surprise model proposed by Macedo and Cardoso. On the other hand, if the strategy failed, the surprise "felt" by the agent would be approximately 0.48 ($Surprise(E_g) = log_2(1 + 0.70 - 0.30)$). As expected and in accordance with the nature of the El Farol problem, considering the fact that it is a strategic environment in which there is no dominant strategy, we did not find high GBS values and consequently GSu values are relatively low.

Second, not surprisingly and in accordance with the literature, we can observe that E3 (green) has "better" results in terms of attendance, CuE, and "good" results in terms of GSu. Attendance oscillates in a narrow range around the capacity of the bar. Higher CuE values means that agents in E3 agents are "feeling" higher happiness than those of E1 and E2. Last but not least, a lower GSu can be considered good because agents are not "feeling" surprised about the actions they choose to take. It means that agents are happier if all use a noise trader strategy (NTS) rather than trying to forecast the next attendance by using a "technical" strategy such as a simple moving average (SMA). However, in real life, it is difficult to imagine a scenario in which a cognitive agent may use a noise strategy to generate the next attendance, just "ignoring" the historical attendance, specifically when we consider the fact that humans intuitively try to discover patterns and predict things, even in random sequences [29, 28].

Third, as we briefly pointed out earlier, regarding *GBS*, the higher values are found in E1, while the lowest values are found in E1. Interestingly, it means that in E1 some agents have a degree of belief that is lower than 0.5. In such situation, we can expect a cognitive agent to change from its current strategy, that he/she believes that is not working $(b(p, t) < 0.5)$, to a new strategy, instead of maintain using it. Therefore, despite the results of E3, the scenario illustrated by E2 as well as its results are more realistic ones.

Nevertheless, it is important to bear in mind that our results were obtained in a particular given setting, with specific configurations, for example, in terms of memory size, belief threhold, process for increasing and decreasing beliefs, and set of strategies available. Perhaps with other configurations the results might be different than ours. This means that, although we do not know which are the preferences of agents and, as expected, we need to make assumptions, relying on some assumptions, such as using the same memory size for all agents, might be a drawback of our approach, especially with respect to yielding results as realistic as possible.

6   Conclusion and Future Work

In this paper, consistent with findings from behavioral economics research and with real life observations, as well as departing from traditional economic theories, we take into account the fact that agents are actually heterogeneous, have bounded rationality, and are not fully rational. In this context, we provided nontrivial insights into the behaviour of agents in such scenarios by using a cognitive modelling approach in the El Farol problem. In three computer experiments we investigated, compared, and discussed a number of features of our agent-based model, specifically the relationship between beliefs and strategies, the emotions of happiness and surprise of cognitive agents, as well as other aspects of market dynamics.

We consider that the current work opens up a novel set of possibilities. We envision at least three future works. First, we could enhance the current work by incorporating more realistic findings with respect to how humans use both memory and past experience in decision-making. For instance, Kahneman and Tversky [13] pointed out that in revising their beliefs, people tend to overweight recent information and underweight prior information, while Griffin and Tversky [12] reported that people update their beliefs based on the "strength" and the "weight" of new evidence, where strength refers to aspects such as the salience and extremity, and weight refers to statistical informativeness such as the sample size. Second, we are interested in testing several processes for increasing and decreasing beliefs, as well as introducing new forms of forgetting (e.g. decay functions), in order to investigate if the results are similar to those we found in the current work. Third, we are interested in applying the ideas and concepts presented in this work to minority games [4] and ultimately to artificial financial markets as well as to compare our results to other cognitive approaches in the same context.

Acknowledgements. This work is supported by a Ph.D. scholarship from Portuguese Foundation for Science and Technology from Ministry of Science, Technology and Higher Education (FCT-MCTES), Portugal, reference SFRH/BD/60700/2009.

References

[1] Arthur, W.B.: Inductive reasoning and bounded rationality. The American Economic Review 84(2), 406–411 (1994)

[2] Baddeley, A., Eysenck, M., Anderson, M.C.: Memory, 1st edn. Psychology Press (February 2009)

[3] Bratman, M., Israel, D., Pollack, M.: Plans and resource-bounded practical reasoning. Computational Intelligence 4(3), 349–355 (1988)

[4] Challet, D., Zhang, Y.C.: Emergence of cooperation and organization in an evolutionary game. Physica A: Statistical and Theoretical Physics 246(3-4), 407–418 (1997)

[5] Challet, D., Marsili, M., Ottino, G.: Shedding light on el farol. Physica A: Statistical Mechanics and its Applications 332, 469–482 (2004)

[6] Chiodo, A., Guidolin, M., Owyang, M.T., Shimoji, M.: Subjective probabilities: psychological evidence and economic applications. Technical report, Federal Reserve Bank of St. Louis (2003)

[7] Cont, R.: Empirical properties of asset returns: stylized facts and statistical issues. Quantitative Finance 1(2), 223 (2001)

[8] Conway, M.A.: Episodic memories. Neuropsychologia 47(11), 2305–2313 (2009)

[9] Cross, R., Grinfeld, M., Lamba, H., Seaman, T.: A threshold model of investor psychology. Physica A: Statistical Mechanics and its Applications 354, 463–478 (2005)

[10] Fama, E.F.: Efficient capital markets: A review of theory and empirical work. The Journal of Finance 25(2), 383–417 (1970)

[11] Farmer, J.D., Foley, D.: The economy needs agent-based modelling. Nature 460(7256), 685–686 (2009)

[12] Griffin, D., Tversky, A.: The weighing of evidence and the determinants of confidence. Cognitive Psychology 24(3), 411–435 (1992)

[13] Kahneman, D., Tversky, A.: Intuitive prediction: Biases and corrective procedures. Management Science 12, 313–327 (1979)

[14] Kahneman, D., Tversky, A.: Prospect theory: An analysis of decision under risk. Econometrica 47(2), 263–291 (1979)

[15] Lazarus, R.S.: Emotion and Adaptation. Oxford University Press, New York (1991)

[16] LeBaron, B.: A builder's guide to agent-based financial markets. Quantitative Finance 1(2), 254 (2001)

[17] Lo, A.W.: The adaptive markets hypothesis: Market efficiency from an evolutionary perspective. Journal of Portfolio Management, 15–29 (2004)

[18] Lorini, E., Castelfranchi, C.: The unexpected aspects of surprise. International Journal of Pattern Recognition and Artificial Intelligence, 817–835 (2006)

[19] Lus, H., AydIn, C.O., Keten, S., Ünsal, H.I., AtIlgan, A.R.: El farol revisited. Physica A: Statistical Mechanics and its Applications 346(3-4), 651–656 (2005)

[20] Lustosa, B.C., Cajueiro, D.O.: Constrained information minority game: How was the night at el farol? Physica A: Statistical Mechanics and its Applications 389(6), 1230–1238 (2010)

[21] Macedo, L.: The Exploration of Unknown Environments by Affective Agents. PhD thesis, University of Coimbra (2006)

[22] Macedo, L., Cardoso, A., Reisenzein, R., Lorini, E., Castelfranchi, C.: Artificial surprise. In: Handbook of Research on Synthetic Emotions and Sociable Robotics: New Applications in Affective Computing and Artificial Intelligence, pp. 267–291 (2009)

[23] Macedo, L., Reisenzein, R., Cardoso, A.: Modeling forms of surprise in artificial agents: empirical and theoretical study of surprise functions. In: 26th Annual Conference of the Cognitive Science Society, pp. 588–593 (2004)

[24] Meyer, W.-U., Reisenzein, R., Schutzwohl, A.: Toward a process analysis of emotions: The case of surprise. Motivation and Emotion 21, 251–274 (1997)

[25] Phelps, S.: Evolutionary Mechanism Design. PhD thesis, University of Liverpool (2007)

[26] Rabin, M.: A perspective on psychology and economics. European Economic Review 46, 657–685 (2002)

[27] Reisenzein, R.: Emotions as metarepresentational states of mind: Naturalizing the belief-desire theory of emotion. Cognitive Systems Research 10(1), 6–20 (2009)

[28] Taleb, N.N.: Fooled by Randomness: The Hidden Role of Chance in Life and in the Markets, 2nd updated edn. Random House (October 2008)

[29] Tversky, A., Kahneman, D.: Judgment under uncertainty: Heuristics and biases. Science 185(4157), 1124–1131 (1974)

Simulation and Performance Assessment of Poker Agents

Luís Filipe Teófilo[1], Rosaldo Rossetti[1], Luís Paulo Reis[2], Henrique Lopes Cardoso[1], and Pedro Alves Nogueira[1]

LIACC – Artificial Intelligence and Computer Science Lab., University of Porto, Portugal
[1] FEUP – Faculty of Engineering, University of Porto – DEI, Portugal
[2] EEUM – School of Engineering, University of Minho – DSI, Portugal
{luis.teofilo,rossetti}@fe.up.pt, lpreis@dsi.uminho.pt,
{hlc,pedro.alves.nogueira}@fe.up.pt

Abstract. The challenge in developing agents for incomplete information games resides in the fact that the maximum utility decision for given information set is not always ascertainable. For large games like Poker, the agents' strategies require opponent modeling, since Nash equilibrium strategies are hard to compute. In light of this, simulation systems are indispensable for accurate assessment of agents' capabilities. Nevertheless, current systems do not accommodate the needs of computer poker research since they were designed mainly as an interface for human players competing against agents. In order to contribute towards improving computer poker research, a new simulation system was developed. This system introduces scientifically unexplored game modes with the purpose of providing a more realistic simulation environment, where the agent must play carefully to manage its initial resources. An evolutionary simulation feature was also included so as to provide support for the improvement of adaptive strategies. The simulator has built-in odds calculation, an agent development API, other platform agents and several variants support and an agent classifier with realistic game indicators including exploitability estimation. Tests and qualitative analysis have proven this simulator to be faster and better suited for thorough agent development and performance assessment.

Keywords: Poker, Simulation, Opponent Modeling, Game Theory, Incomplete Information Games, Exploitability, Agent Validation, Gamblers ruin.

1 Introduction

Games research is a popular subfield of AI research since there are many games that were and still are an interesting challenge for AI. Classic games such as chess or checkers served as a test-bed to solve many defying problems and significant results were achieved – a computer program defeated human experts [5, 10].

Because games have a limited set of well-defined rules, studying them allows for easy testing of a new approach, making it possible to accurately measure its degree of success. This is done by comparing results of many games played against programs based on other approaches or against human players, meaning that games have a well-defined metric for measuring the development progress. It is then possible to determine with more accuracy whether the solution is optimal to solve a given problem.

F. Giardini and F. Amblard (Eds.): MABS 2012, LNAI 7838, pp. 69–84, 2013.

Also, the fact that games have a "recreational dimension" and great importance for the entertainment industry today motivates further research in this domain.

1.1 Incomplete Information Games

Incomplete information games (IIG) have indistinguishable game states. This means that for a given information set there is a least two possible game states. As the agent does not know the actual game state (only possible states) it usually uses a mixed strategy: it assigns a probability to each possible action by the opponent. The probability of each action depends both on the probability of reaching an advantageous game state and on the strategy the agent assumes that the opponent is using – opponent modeling. For large games such as Poker, with 10^{18} possible information sets it is currently unfeasible to create a best response strategy[1]. For this reason, when constructing opponent models, the agents use abstracted information sets – treating a group of information sets the same way, reflecting on an equal strategy for all of them. This way, it is possible to reduce the complexity of the game to compute abstracted best response strategies [9].

1.2 Why Poker?

Poker caught the interest of the AI research community on the last decade. This IIG presents a radically different challenge when compared to other games like Chess, where both players are always aware of the full state of the game. This means that in Chess it is possible to somehow understand the opponent's strategy by observing the pieces movement. Conversely, Poker's game state is hidden: each player can only see his/her cards and the community cards[2]. Thus, it is much more difficult to understand players' strategies since the only chance to observe the game state is at the end of the game and only if the players choose to display their cards. Poker is also a stochastic game, i.e. it admits the element of chance since the players' cards are randomly dealt.

1.3 Simulation System Scope

New Computer Poker developments are made through the implementation of software agents. A Poker agent is software that replaces a human in the task of playing Poker, by taking decisions without any intervention. Since playing Poker can be considered a repetitive task for a human player, the development of agents allows professional players to be rewarded for their effective know-how of the game and not by their physical endurance or patience. This is true, because most lucrative players are usually the ones that play more carefully and more games.

It is important to measure the level of competitiveness of a Poker agent to check if its results improved compared to those of past approaches. This is usually done

---

[1] Best response strategy – strategy that maximizes utility against a given opponent.
[2] Community card – visible card that is shared by all players.

through simulation systems that run a series of games following the rules of Poker. However certain features can be introduced in the simulated environment to speed-up the simulation; for instance, by introducing table seat permutation [24] the variance of the results can be reduced, therefore resulting in less iterations.

Current simulation systems (see subsection 3.1) are not suited for research projects because they present problems such as being slow or having an architecture that does not easily support the creation of new agents. They also do not explore important aspects of the game like bankroll[3] management, which is considered essential by Poker professionals. The importance of bankroll management can be explained by the gamblers ruin theorem [8]. This theorem states that even if players use a strategy that has positive expected value[4], they will still be very likely to be bankrupt if they raise the stakes[5] when they win but do not lower them when they lose.

1.4   New Simulation System Goals

In order to overcome the limitations found in previously developed Poker simulators, a new simulator has been created which aims to integrate the most important features present in other simulators with new features that will certainly lead Computer Poker research into new directions. The requirements of the new simulation system are:

— An easily expandable architecture to support the creation of new agents or the introduction of new game variants. This includes an agent development API.
— New game modes such as ring, which allow researchers to explore the paradigm of bankroll management.
— Evolutionary simulation of Poker games which encourages studies about strategy evolution through the principle of natural selection. This feature is not known to be natively supported by any Poker simulator.
— A set of validation tools that allow for a quick and precise assessment of the agent capabilities to predict their performance in different real-life environments.

1.5   Structure

This paper is a revised version of [17] and is organized as follows. Section 2 briefly introduces this paper's background by presenting the Computer Poker domain. Section 3 describes recent related work on Computer Poker by enumerating the most relevant agents and simulation systems currently in use. Section 4 shows how Poker players were modeled in the current simulator. Section 5 presents the overall architecture of the system and its key features. Section 6 describes the agent assessment methodology used by this system. Section 7 compares this system against previously developed systems through benchmark tests and a qualitative analysis. Finally, some conclusions and future research recommendations are discussed in section 8.

---

[3] Bankroll – amount of money that a given player reserved for playing Poker.
[4] Expected value – average amount of money won per play.
[5] Stake – amount of betted money per game.

2   Background

Poker is a generic name for hundreds of games with similar rules [16], called variants. This work is mainly focused on the Texas Hold'em variant, which is probably the most popular nowadays. Hold'em rules also have specific characteristics that allow for new developed approaches to be adapted to other variants with reduced effort [1].

The game is based upon the concept of players betting that their current hand[6] is stronger than the hands of their opponents. All bets throughout the game are placed in the pot and, at the end of the game, the player with the highest ranked hand wins. Alternatively, it is also possible to win the game by forcing the opponents to fold their hands by making bets that they are not willing to match. Thus, since the opponents' cards are hidden it is possible to win the game with a hand with lower score. This is done by convincing the opponents that one's hand is the highest ranked one.

2.1   Rules of Texas Hold'em

Texas Hold'em Poker is a community card Poker variant. In each game there is a minimum bet and at the start two cards are dealt for every player – pocket cards. A dealer player is assigned and marked with a dealer button. The dealer position rotates clockwise from game to game. After that, the player on the left of the dealer position posts the small blind (half of the minimum bet) and the player on his left posts the big blind (minimum bet). The first player to act is the one on the left of the big blind.

The game is composed of four rounds: Pre-Flop, Flop, Turn and River. The participants play in turns and they can match the highest bet (Call), increase that bet (Raise) or forfeit the game and lose the pot (Fold). A player wins if he/she is the last standing player or if he/she has the highest ranked card after the last round (River). This Poker variant has two sub-variants with a small difference in their rule set. These are called Limit and No Limit Texas Hold'em. The main difference between them is the existence of a bet value limit.

2.2   Hand Score

A Poker hand is a set of five cards that define the player's score. Let Δ be the set of all cards, Φ the set of pocket cards and Ω the set of community cards so that Φ, $\Omega \subseteq \Delta$. Thus, the score function can be defined as $s: [\Delta]^5 \rightarrow$ and a player's score R is such that:

$$R = \max(\{s(x): x \in [\Phi \cup \Omega]^5\}) \tag{1}$$

The possible hand ranks are (from stronger to weaker): Straight Flush (sequence of same suit), Four of a Kind (4 cards with same rank), Full House (Three of a Kind + Pair), Flush (5 cards with same suit), Straight (sequence), Three of a Kind (3 cards with same rank), Two Pair, One Pair (2 cards with same rank) and Highest Card (not qualifying to other ranks). Examples of each rank are demonstrated in table 1.

---

[6] Hand – best possible set of player and community cards.

Table 1. Examples of Poker hand scores

Royal Flush	A♠	K♠	Q♠	J♠	T♠	Straight Flush	8♥	7♥	6♥	5♥	4♥
Four of a Kind	7♣	7♦	7♥	7♠	8♠	Full House	A♣	A♠	A♥	Q♥	Q♦
Flush	A♦	J♦	8♦	5♦	3♦	Straight	A♣	2♣	3♠	4♠	5♠
Three of a Kind	7♣	7♦	7♥	A♣	3♦	Two pairs	3♣	3♠	7♠	7♥	Q♠
One pair	2♠	2♣	8♣	7♣	3♥	High Card	A♥	T♥	4♦	3♣	2♣

3   Related Work

In order to build the system described in this paper, several Poker simulators
were tested and analyzed so as to identify the lacking features. This system was also
designed to provide tools to support agent validation, and thus the most relevant approaches on agent creation were studied. Finally, some methods for efficient probability calculation in Poker were consulted, since agents' decisions must be taken rapidly.

3.1   Poker Simulation Systems

A Poker Simulator is any software whose purpose is to test agents against other
agents or human players, in order to predict the agent's success at long term. A brief
description of the main simulators is presented next.

AAAI Competition Server. The AAAI Poker Server is an application made to simulate thousands of games between poker agents. This application is used to determine
the winner of the Annual Poker Bot Competition organized by University Of Alberta
[24]. This simulator is very simple and lacks personalization options.

Poker Academy. One of the best resources for testing a Poker agent is the simulation
software named Poker Academy [7]. In this simulator it is possible to compete against
the best agents developed by the Computer Poker Research Group at the University of
Alberta. It was launched in December 2003 as a tool for professional player training.
Poker Academy provides a Java based API (named the Meerkat API) that allows
Computer Poker researchers to plug in their own custom agents. The program also
keeps track of all the hands played and can display comprehensive charts and analysis
of the player statistics over time. A problem of Poker Academy is that it is misfit for
extensive simulations, because of the heavy user interface that results in low simulation speeds. Another problem is that it is not possible to start a simulation without a
human player, which means that in each simulation there will always be an additional
ghost player that the user must configure to always fold his hands, adulterating for
this reason the simulation results.

Meerkat Open Testbed. Open Meerkat Poker Testbed [15] is an open source implementation of the Meerkat API for running Poker games. It imitates the Poker Academy
simulator; however it is much faster because it has a light weighted user interface. This
application supports Fixed/No-Limit cash games with automatic rebuy. It generates
bankroll evolution plots, implements seat permutation to reduce game variance (replay
games with same cards but with different seat order) and generates game logs. It also

shows an online bankroll evolution chart. The main problem of this simulator is that it currently only supports cash games and between 2, 3, 4 or 6 players. Another problem is that it only presents one plot type: the evolution of the players' chips through time.

Other Simulation Systems. One of the recent trends to develop Poker agents is the use of evolutionary computation [12], i.e., algorithms based on the biological principle of natural selection. Until now, there is no known Poker simulation system that natively supports evolutionary simulation.

3.2   Current Poker Agents

First approaches to build Poker agents were rule-based, which involves specifying the action that should be taken for a given information set [2]. The next approaches were based on simulation techniques like [3], i.e. generating random instances in order to obtain a statistical average and decide the action. These approaches led to the creation of agents that were able to defeat weak human opponents.

The great breakthrough in Computer Poker research was the discovery of the Counter Factual Regret Minimization Algorithm (CFR) in [23]. The CFR algorithm allows for the computation of a Nash Equilibrium strategy in large games like Poker through self-play[7]. This could be done before through linear programming methods (like Simplex) but CFR is much faster because the processing time is proportional to the number of information sets instead of to the number of game states (about 6 orders of magnitude less). Several approaches based on CFR, like Restricted Nash Response [10] and Data-biased response [11] backed the first victories against Poker experts up.

Other recent methodologies were based on pattern matching [21, 22], Monte Carlo Search Tree algorithm [4], reinforcement learning [18] and case based reasoning [13]. More recent works are described in the reviews [14, 19].

Despite all the breakthroughs achieved, there is no known approach in which the agent has reached a level similar to a competent human player.

3.3   Poker Hand Odds Calculation

Evaluating the odds of a hand consists of measuring its quality in a round of the game. By evaluating the hand it is possible to determine the probability of winning or losing the current game. Using this knowledge the agent can decide to either fold the hand or play it, based on the probability of success and the risk level [20]. The process to calculate the winning probability of a hand is described on Figure 1.

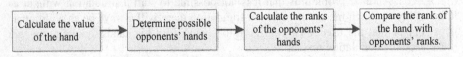

Fig. 1. Poker hand odds calculation process

The key parts of this process are the calculation of the value of a hand and the determination of the opponents' possible hands.

---

[7] Self-play – an agent playing against itself or against an agent with an equal strategy.

Calculating the value of a hand (corresponding to the *s* function in equation 1) is not trivial in Poker. The best known solution is the *TwoPlusTwo* Evaluator which is based on the usage of pre-computed tables [20] which can quickly provide the value of the hand. The high speed of this method is very relevant since the number of possible opponent hands is usually very high. The drawback of this evaluator is that the pre-computed table is heavy in memory usage.

There are other processes to calculate the odds of a hand based on the Hand Strength algorithm. The hand strength is the probability of the current hand being the best if the game reaches a showdown[8] with all remaining players. Using section 2.2 terminology, the hand strength (*HS*) for a given number of opponents *n* is given by:

$$Remain = [\Delta \backslash \Phi]^5$$
$$Ahead = |\{s(x) > R : x \in Remain\}|$$
$$Tied = |\{s(x) = R : x \in Remain\}|$$
$$Behind = |\{s(x) < R : x \in Remain\}| \tag{2}$$
$$HS_n = \left(\frac{Ahead + {Tied}/{2}}{Ahead + Tied + Behind} \right)^n$$

The main problem of Hand Strength is that it does not address the possibility of the hand improving in subsequent rounds of the game, which is possible because in Poker new cards are revealed at the start of every round. This issue is addressed by the Hand Potential Formula [20] which sums up possible hand strengths in subsequent rounds. Another issue is that Hand Strength only works for sets of at least 5 cards. An alternative to this is the Chen Formula [6], that computes the relative value of pocket hands.

4   Texas Hold'em Player Modeling

The simulation system described in this paper uses a multi-agent architecture where an agent represents a Poker player. Many types of agents were created for this simulation platform, each one of them deployed by an object class. The way each class relates to others is depicted in the following UML class diagram (Figure 2).

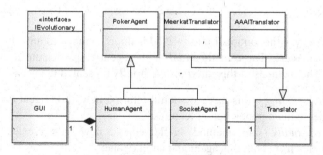

Fig. 2. Poker Agents class model

---

[8] Showdown – last round of Poker where players show their cards and the winner is decided.

Poker Agent – it is an abstract class based on the Meerkat API [7] that represents any agent on the system. The class contains a set of abstract methods that represent the events that each agent has to answer to during the simulation. Thus, to create an agent that works in this system it is necessary to extend this class. Agents must implement a set of methods corresponding to events of the game:

- *pocketCards(Card[], Seat)* – occurs when the agent receives its pocket cards.
- *observeAction(GameInfo)* – the main routine of the agent. It is called when the agent is requested to perform an action.
- *actionEvent(Seat, Action)* – A player in a given seat has performed an action.
- *winEvent(Seat, Amount, Card[])* – A player in a given seat has won an amount of chips with a given hand.
- *showdownEvent(Seat, Card[])* – player in a given seat has shown his cards.
- *gameOverEvent()* – the current game is now over.

HumanAgent – this agent extends the class PokerAgent and redirects the game events to a graphical user interface (GUI). This GUI is controlled by a human player. Thus, this class represents a form of interaction between human and artificial players.

SocketAgent – the socket agent is responsible for communicating with external agents developed for other simulation platforms. This way, any external agent from Poker Academy [7] or AAAI Server [24] can be used in this simulator with no need of re-writing, using the new *PokerAgent* class. The communication process is demonstrated in Figure 3. When a *SocketAgent* receives a request, it chooses the correct translator and then sends a translated request via sockets to an external application that is linked to the external agent. The external agent then sends the response all the way back to the *SocketAgent* and then the *SocketAgent* plays accordingly.

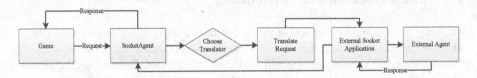

Fig. 3. Communication between the Socket Agent and the External agent

IEvolutionary – this optional interface adds three methods to any class that inherits from *PokerAgent*. These methods allow the agent to participate in evolutionary simulations. The methods of this interface are briefly presented below:

— *ReproduceAsexually* – this method should return a new child agent created by the current one, with upgraded parent features;
— *ReproduceSexually* – this method should return a new agent created by crossing characteristics from both this agent and another one;
— *Fitness* – this method returns a number that measures the level of adaptation of the agent to the current environment. The fitness could be for instance the average expected value against all opponents.

5   Simulation System Architecture

This section describes both the overall architecture of the simulation system and its novel features.

5.1   Overview

The architecture of the simulator is depicted in Figure 4.

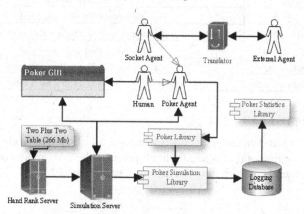

Fig. 4. Poker Simulation System Architecture

The simulator is composed of the following components:

— Hand Rank Server – a server that is used to calculate the rank of the Poker hands based on the algorithms described in section 2.2;
— Simulation Server/Poker Simulation Library – the application that is responsible for simulating Poker games;
— Logging database – all agent moves are registered in a database for future profiling and result analysis;
— Poker Agent – this entity represents an abstract Poker agent (see Section 4);
— Poker Library – definition of general Poker data structures;
— Poker Statistics library – calculates statistical indicators and thus validates agents;
— Poker GUI – user-friendly GUI to allow humans to play against the agents.

5.2   Hand Rank Server

The hand rank server is a process that runs concurrently with the simulation server and that evaluates Poker hands for all agents. This was created to save memory since the fastest hand evaluating algorithm – TwoPlusTwo Evaluator [20] – must load a 266 MB table. If each agent were to load the table individually it would be problematic in terms of memory usage, especially on the evolutionary simulation module where thousands of agents might be needed.

The hand ranking server uses a simple UDP communication protocol to provide different measures that evaluate the chance of winning: hand rank; hand strength; hand potential; effective hand strength and Chen formula. Table 2 presents the commands that can be sent to the server (The <Hand> is a string composed of 5 to 7 cards like 'AsAd7s4d2c'). Already computed results can be optionally saved by the hand ranking server in a private database in order to speed up future requests.

Table 2. Hand Ranking Server Commands

Command	Description
RANK <Hand>	Retrieves the rank of the hand.
HS <Hand> <NO>	Retrieves the hand's strength. <NO> = remaining adversaries.
HP <Hand> <NO>	Retrieves the hand's potential.
EHS <Hand> <NO>	Retrieves the effective hand strength.
CHEN <Card> <Card>	Retrieves the relative value of a hand with 2 cards.

5.3   Logging Database

The simulator has a database that contains records of all moves made by registered players, if the logging option is set. Figure 5 presents the class model of the database that was subsequently converted to a relational database model.

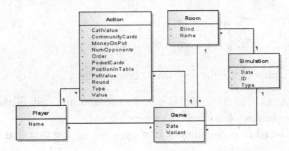

Fig. 5. Game moves database class model

The database uses a data warehouse model which will help researchers process the raw data. This produces some intentional redundancy in the data, namely the link between the Player and the Game classes that can be used to facilitate game analysis, reporting and data mining. The model is composed by the following classes:

— Action – represents an action in a given game performed by a player. This class represents the star table and thereby a key aspect of the simulator database. An action presents the full state of the game table when it took place, instead of only containing the action type and the value;
— Game – represents a game which is a set of actions;
— Player – represents a registered player in the game;
— Simulation – represents a simulation run on a date and time. It is a set of consecutive games;
— Room – some simulation modes described in Subsection 5.4 require the concept of room/table i.e. the occurrence of games in parallel in the same simulation.

The used format is also helpful for case based reasoning agents, because of the presence of redundancy on the action table that aids the computation of approximate information sets [13].

5.4   Poker Simulation Module (Poker Simulation Library)

This module is responsible for performing the simulation itself. When the simulation starts the user will be asked which players will be part of the game, which simulation mode to use and which Poker rules. The class diagram on Figure 6 shows the entity structure of the simulation module. The existence of simulation modes is one of the innovative aspects of the system and five different modes were considered.

Simple Tournament – a simple tournament is a set of games that only ends when only one player remains. This kind of simulation allows testing the capabilities of the agent to manage its cash and the blind increase in order to win the tournament and avoid the gamblers ruin theorem [8].

Full Tournament – this mode is similar to a simple tournament but with several gaming tables.

Cash Games – the common type of simulation that is used to validate Poker Agents. It consists of a finite set of games with static blinds[9] and player money reset at the beginning of each game. To reduce the variance of the results, table seat permutations is used – for each game positions are switch and the same cards are dealt, so everyone has equal chances. This type of simulation allows players to be tested on the long run, always on equal footing.

Ring Games – this mode is similar to what happens in online casinos. The agent starts with a given amount of chips and must manage it in order to survive. In addition, the agent should choose the table that contains opponents that are more susceptible to its strategy and tables with blinds that do not present a risk of quickly losing all cash.

Evolutionary Cash Games – this mode is similar to cash games simulation. However, in this mode, from time to time, natural selection is applied. This means that the agents with less fitness will be discarded and the other agents will reproduce, creating child agents that contain characteristics of both parents.

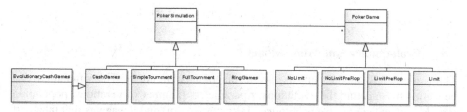

Fig. 6. Poker simulation module

---

[9] Blinds – minimum bets placed by two players at the start of the game.

There are four main game types: Limit Texas Hold'em, No Limit Texas Hold'em, Limit Texas Hold'em Only Pre-Flop and No Limit Texas Hold'em Only Pre-Flop. The innovative part of the game types is the presence of "Only Pre-Flop" variants. These are variants of Texas Hold'em that only last until the Flop round therefore they do not have community cards. This variant is popular among new Poker researchers, given the much lower number of information sets than in full Texas Hold'em resulting in less abstraction for strategy computation.

For the same reason, the variant Khun Poker was also included. Khun Poker is a variant that only uses 3 to 13 cards (the number of card is a simulation parameter) and no community cards, resulting in a maximum number of 52 possible information sets. This allows researchers to quickly validate new approaches, with much less effort and computation time needed, especially when working with algorithms such as CFR that can take weeks to finish for full Texas Hold'em.

5.5   User Interface

In order to quickly configure the simulation parameters, a configuration GUI was developed (figure 7). This GUI includes an optional and minimalist 2D visualizer to observe the agents in action.

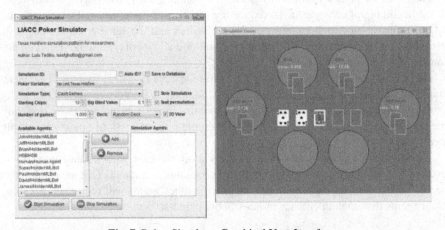

Fig. 7. Poker Simulator Graphical User Interface

5.6   Evolutionary Simulation Model

The evolutionary model follows as the diagram on figure 8. The simulation can be started by selecting the evolutionary parameters (number of iterations, population size: M, percentage of agents eliminated per iteration: n) and the agents that take part on the simulation. The population size is maintained throughout the simulation but it is renewed on every iteration. The simulation ends after a defined number of iterations.

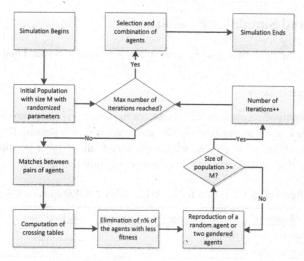

Fig. 8. Evolutionary simulation module

6   Agent Assessment

After performing the simulations, the statistics module can be used to analyze the results. Three types of statistics were included:

Bankroll evolution – the evolution of the player cash during the simulation. This statistic shows the evolution of the agents' profit during a simulation.

Player indicators evolution – several indicators used by Poker experts are available in evolution plots and described on table 3.

Exploitability analysis – the exploitability is the agent's utility against a best response agent. A best response agent is the average best possible strategy against one's own strategy. Calculating a best response can be done using CFR. Since Poker is a very large game, abstraction is needed to perform this operation in a timely manner.

This simulator provides exploitability computation by following the next steps:

— Selection of the level of card abstraction (0 to 100). The results are more accurate for lower levels of abstraction.
— Selection of the level of action sequence abstraction (0 to 100).
— Selection of the number of iterations for CFR and for final simulation.
— Computation of the best response strategy using the CFR algorithm with a desired level of abstraction;
— Final simulation and computation of the exploitability level.

Table 3. Player statistical indicators

Indicator	Description	Round
VPIP	Percentage of games where the player puts money in the pot.	Pre-Flop
PFR	Number of Raises / (Number of Calls + Number of Folds)	Pre-Flop
AF	Number of Raises / Number of Calls	Flop

7   Tests and Simulator Evaluation

The developed simulator was tested against other simulators in speed and features.

7.1   Benchmark Tests

In order to compare the speed of this simulator against previously developed simulators, a benchmark test was performed. The test consisted in repeating for 1.000 tries a simulation of 100.000 cash games, with 4 players without table permutation (since Poker Academy does not support it). The results are shown in table 4.

Table 4. Benchmark test results for 1.000 tries with 100.000 games and 4 players

Simulator	Average Time (seconds)	Std. Deviation (seconds)
Open Meerkat Test Bed [6]	43,0	6,3
Poker Academy [5]	660,3	48,7
This Simulator	27,7	1,8

As can be observed, the simulator described in this paper is the fastest one. The results were very close to the Open Meerkat Testbed, however the Poker Academy simulator was much slower. This was due to the heavy user interface present in the Poker Academy software that slowed down the simulation process.

7.2   Qualitative Comparision

Table 5 summarizes the comparision between the main Poker simulators. The simulator described in this paper presents almost every feature of the other two.

Table 5. Poker Simulators Comparision table

Feature	This Simulator	Open Meerkat	Poker Academy	Is Key Feature?
2D visualizer	Yes, Simple	No	Yes	No
Agent Development API	Yes	Yes	Yes	Yes
Bankroll Analysis	Simple	Simple	Complete	Yes
Card Rank Computation	Yes	No	Partially	Yes
Database support	Yes	No	?	No
Evolutionary Simulation	Yes	No	No	Yes
Expansible Architecture	Yes	Yes	No	Yes
Exploitability	Yes	No	No	Yes
Human players	Yes	No	Yes	No
Logging	Yes	Yes	Yes	Yes
Online play	No	No	Yes	No
Pre-developed agents	No	Yes, Simple	Yes	Yes
Simulation Speed	Fast	Fast	Slow	Yes
Table seat permutation	Yes	Yes	No	Yes
Former agent support	Yes	No	No	No

The only missing features are online play and pre-developed agents. Despite this simulator not providing pre-developed agents, this can be balanced by the *"Former Agent Support feature"* which allows the use of agents developed for other platforms.

8   Conclusions

This paper presented a new system for Poker simulation that is scalable, fast and able to lead Computer Poker research to unexplored paths. The key features of this system are the possibility of performing evolutionary simulations, tournament simulation and support for external agents. Also, this simulation system provides access to an extensive database that could be easily used for data-mining and better opponent modeling profiling in the future. Moreover, there could be significant improvement of agents' performance in real-life environments by analyzing the comprehensive statistical indicators generated by the system.

This simulator is in final stages of development, with some extensive testing already done. Performance tests demonstrated that this simulator is faster than all the others it was tested against. The qualititative analysis also shows that this simulator outperforms previously developed simulators in terms of research aiding features and proper agent assessment. In future work this simulating system shall be used to help the development and test of Poker agents in order to allow them to participate in the annual Computer Poker Competition as well as in games against human players.

Acknowledgments. This work was supported by Fundação para a Ciência e a Tecnologia for providing the Ph.D. Scholarship SFRH/BD/71598/2010.

References

1. Billings, D.: Computer Poker. University of Alberta (1995)
2. Billings, D., et al.: Opponent modeling in poker. In: Proceedings of the National Conference on Artificial Intelligence, pp. 493–499. John Wiley & Sons Ltd. (1998)
3. Billings, D., et al.: Using selective-sampling simulations in poker. In: AAAI Syring Symposium Search Techniques for Problem Solving Under Uncertainty and Incomplete Information, pp. 1–6 (1999)
4. Van den Broeck, G., Driessens, K., Ramon, J.: Monte-Carlo Tree Search in Poker Using Expected Reward Distributions. In: Zhou, Z.-H., Washio, T. (eds.) ACML 2009. LNCS, vol. 5828, pp. 367–381. Springer, Heidelberg (2009)
5. Campbell, M., et al.: Deep Blue. Artificial Intelligence 134(1-2), 57–83 (2002)
6. Chen, B., Ankenman, J.: The Mathematics of Poker. Conjelco (2006)
7. Davidson, A., et al.: Poker Academy Pro - The Ultimate Poker Software, http://www.poker-academy.com/
8. Epstein, R.A.: The Theory of Gambling and Statistical Logic. Academic Press Inc. (1995)
9. Gilpin, A., Sandholm, T.: Better automated abstraction techniques for imperfect information games, with application to Texas Hold'em poker. In: Proceedings of the 6th International Joint Conference on Autonomous Agents and Multiagent Systems, AAMAS 2007, p. 1. ACM Press (2007)

10. Johanson, M.: Robust Strategies and Counter-Strategies: Building a Champion Level Computer Poker Player. University of Alberta (2007)
11. Johanson, M., Bowling, M.: Data biased robust counter strategies. In: Proceedings of the Twelfth International Conference on Artificial Intelligence and Statistics (AISTATS), pp. 264–271 (2009)
12. Quek, H., et al.: Evolving Nash-optimal poker strategies using evolutionary computation. Frontiers of Computer Science in China 3(1), 73–91 (2009)
13. Rubin, J., Watson, I.: Case-based strategies in computer poker. AI Communications 25(1), 19–48 (2012)
14. Rubin, J., Watson, I.: Computer poker: A review. Artificial Intelligence 175(5-6), 958–987 (2011)
15. Schatzberg, D.: Open Meerkat Bot Simulation Testbed, http://code.google.com/p/opentestbed/
16. Sklansky, D.: The Theory of Poker: A Professional Poker Player Teaches You How to Think Like One. Two Plus Two (2007)
17. Teófilo, L.F., et al.: A Simulation System to Support Computer Poker Research. In: 13th International Workshop on Multi-Agent Based Simulation at AAMAS Workshop Proceedings, València, pp. 81–92 (2012)
18. Teófilo, L.F., Passos, N., Reis, L.P., Cardoso, H.L.: Adapting Strategies to Opponent Models in Incomplete Information Games: A Reinforcement Learning Approach for Poker. In: Kamel, M., Karray, F., Hagras, H. (eds.) AIS 2012. LNCS, vol. 7326, pp. 220–227. Springer, Heidelberg (2012)
19. Teófilo, L.F., et al.: Computer Poker Research at LIACC. In: Computer Poker Symposium. AAAI (2012)
20. Teófilo, L.F.: Estimating the Probability of Winning for Texas Hold'em Poker Agents. In: Proceedings of the 6th Doctoral Symposium on Informatics Engineering, pp. 129–140 (2011)
21. Teófilo, L.F., Reis, L.P.: Building a No Limit Texas Hold'em Poker Agent based on Game Logs using Supervised Learning. In: Kamel, M., Karray, F., Gueaieb, W., Khamis, A. (eds.) AIS 2011. LNCS (LNAI), vol. 6752, pp. 73–82. Springer, Heidelberg (2011)
22. Teófilo, L.F., Reis, L.P.: HoldemML: A framework to generate No Limit Hold'em Poker agents from human player strategies. In: 6th Iberian Conference on Information Systems and Technologies (CISTI 2011), pp. 755–760. IEEE (2011)
23. Zinkevich, M., et al.: A new algorithm for generating equilibria in massive zero-sum games. In: Proceedings of the 22nd National Conference on Artificial intelligence, AAAI 2007, vol. 1, pp. 788–793 (2007)
24. Zinkevich, M., Littman, M.L.: The 2006 AAAI Computer Poker Competition. Journal of International Computer Games Association 29, 166–167 (2006)

EGTAOnline: An Experiment Manager for Simulation-Based Game Studies

Ben-Alexander Cassell and Michael P. Wellman

Computer Science & Engineering
University of Michigan
Ann Arbor, MI 48109-2121 USA

Abstract. Empirical game-theoretic analysis (EGTA) is a promising methodology for studying complex strategic scenarios through agent-based simulation. One challenge of utilizing this methodology is that it can require tremendous amounts of computation. Constructing the payoff matrix for a game of even moderate complexity entails significant data gathering and management concerns. We present EGTAOnline, an experiment management system that simplifies the application of the EGTA methodology to large games. We describe the architecture of EGTAOnline, explain why such a tool is practically important, and discuss avenues of research that are suggested through the use of EGTAOnline.

1 Introduction

From university-operated clusters to Amazon EC2 (`aws.amazon.com`), researchers increasingly have access to large pools of machines to aid in computational experimentation. Large-scale computing is increasingly available and inexpensive, yet human capital costs remain quite high. Researchers wishing to exploit available computational resources typically must learn the technologies for distributing and scheduling the computation, as well as tools for managing the copious amounts of data being created (Sheutz and Harris, 2012). Learning how to leverage distributed computing is often orthogonal to one's research goals, leading to a tradeoff between convenience and limitations on problem scale.

It is hard to quantify how these human capital costs impinge on research production. We can see only what research was produced, not what research might have been conducted had convenient tools been available. Experimenters may unduly limit the scope of studies, for example by capping problem instances at the size tractable for their desktop computers. Such restrictions may detract from the real-world relevance of computational investigations, or otherwise diminish the value of published studies.

Scope limitations can significantly weaken conclusions in the analysis of *empirical games*: game-theoretic models induced from simulations of multiagent interactions. In contrast to other forms of agent-based modeling, empirical game-theoretic analysis (EGTA) addresses the question of strategy selection by comparing the payoffs obtained when agents play different configurations of strategies in simulation. As for any game model, an empirical game maps *strategy profiles*

F. Giardini and F. Amblard (Eds.): MABS 2012, LNAI 7838, pp. 85–100, 2013.

(joint strategy configurations) of the agents (*players*, in game theory terminology) to payoff values representing the utility accrued by the respective agent for playing its strategy in that profile. The space of profiles grows exponentially with the numbers of players and strategies, pushing the construction of games of even moderate complexity beyond the reach of a typical desktop computer. Even if a single computer were fast enough to conduct the vast amounts of necessary simulation, the researcher may still experience data management concerns as storing all the observation data in memory will quickly impinge on the resources required to run further simulation, bringing the process of data acquisition to a grinding halt. As such, some mechanism for managing the distribution of game simulations and the retrieval of observations is needed.

We present EGTAOnline, an experiment management system designed to make studying large empirical games, derived from agent-based simulations, more convenient. Our current implementation of EGTAOnline strives to make the most common aspects of employing the empirical game-theoretic analysis methodology available through simple web forms, while supporting more complex functionality through a JSON (www.json.org) API.

Following a review of related efforts, we present the EGTA methodology and detail how the EGTAOnline architecture supports the application of this methodology. Afterwards, we discuss how EGTAOnline supports iterative experimentation through data reuse, and how the scheduling API enables automated game refinement, leading to new areas of research. Finally, we describe the usage of our system to date.

2   Related Work

Many previous efforts have aimed to take advantage of distributed computing for agent-based simulation. One thread of discussion centers on *agent-level parallelism* and how to efficiently distribute a multi-agent based simulation (MABS) over multiple compute nodes. Riley and Riley (2003) presented a system for distributed execution of MABS that limits the effect of varying network and system loads on simulation by ensuring that agents are always given sufficient time to think, extending the causal ordering constraints of an earlier parallel and distributed discrete-event simulation environment. Mengistu et al. (2008) identified several architectural issues in designing MABS for grid computing, including threading and communication overhead, and presented middleware to address some of these challenges. Alberts et al. (2012) demonstrated that the parallelism afforded by modern graphics cards can be useful for simulations with millions of agents, as may be necessary when simulating biological systems. In contrast, *simulation-level parallelism*, as employed for example by Bononi et al. (2005), distributes simulation runs, possibly with differing run-time parameters, across multiple compute nodes. EGTAOnline likewise applies parallelism at the simulation level, and exploits the flexibility of specifying different run-time parameters to simulate multiple strategy profiles in parallel. Game simulation is particularly amenable to the exploitation of simulation-level parallelism as profile observations are independent and the number of profiles to observe is tremendous.

EGTAOnline builds on a tradition of tool-building in the computational game theory community. McKelvey et al. (2006) described Gambit, a collection of game-specification tools and analysis algorithms. GAMUT (Nudelman et al., 2004) offers functions for generating random instances from an extensive set of game classes. Both of these toolkits support analytically specified games, whereas EGTAOnline is built to address the construction of game models from simulation data. EGTAOnline was also inspired by two existing systems, developed by Jordan et al. (2007) and Collins et al. (2009), that provided web interfaces for scheduling simulations of a supply chain management game. Our current system was motivated in part by scheduling and data management issues that arose while conducting EGTA studies of the equity premium in financial markets (Cassell and Wellman, 2012) and wireless access point selection (Cassell et al., 2011). It became clear that an experiment manager with the capabilities described here would have greatly facilitated that work.

3   Empirical Game-Theoretic Analysis

Empirical game-theoretic analysis (Wellman, 2006) applies the analytical tools of game theory to games that are constructed from empirical observations of strategic play. These observations may come from real-world data or from agent-based simulation. The EGTAOnline system supports development of empirical game models induced from simulation.

Formally, a normal-form game Γ is specified by the tuple $\langle I, \{S_i\}, u(\cdot) \rangle$. In this description, I is the set of players of the game and S_i is the set of strategies that player $i \in I$ may play. A profile of Γ, $s = (s_1, \ldots, s_{|I|})$, assigns a strategy to each player. Players may adopt a *mixed strategy*, a probability distribution over playing each of the strategies in their strategy set. When one or more players adopt a mixed-strategy, the joint-strategy selection is referred to as a *mixed-strategy profile*, and is otherwise referred to as a *pure-strategy profile*. The function $u(\cdot)$ maps a pure-strategy profile of Γ to the payoff each player receives for playing its assigned strategy in the profile, $(u_1(s), \ldots, u_{|I|}(s))$. This description implies an $|I|$-dimensional payoff matrix, where entries are payoff vectors in $\mathbb{R}^{|I|}$, indexed by the corresponding profile. Player utilities for a mixed-strategy profile are calculated by taking the expectation of payoffs achieved under the pure-strategy profiles that can be realized under that mixed-strategy profile.

We can often achieve a more compact game model by exploiting symmetry in the set of players. A *role-symmetric game* is a tuple $\Gamma = \langle \{I_j\}, \{S_j\}, u(\cdot) \rangle$, where the set of players are partitioned into roles such that players in role j all have the strategy set S_j. Role symmetry also constrains $u(\cdot)$ such that if two players in a role swap strategies, then their entries in the payoff vector are swapped and all other payoff entries are unaffected. As such, a player's payoff may depend only on its strategy choice, role membership, and how many players of each role play each strategy, being invariant to which of the players within a given role play those strategies. Role-symmetric games provide a natural model for many settings where agents can be partitioned into meaningful categories, such as buyers and sellers in a market, or attackers and defenders in a security game. Assuming role symmetry is without loss of generality, as a game with no symmetry can be expressed by assigning each player its own role. At the other end of the spectrum, a fully symmetric game is one where all players have the same role. Between these two extremes are games with multiple roles, and multiple players in some or all roles.

Game models are used to predict agent behavior through the specification of a *solution concept*, a rule for calculating the probability that each pure-strategy profile will be played. The solution concept that is predominantly adopted in game-theoretic analysis is the *Nash equilibrium*. A Nash equilibrium is a (potentially mixed-strategy) profile such that no player can improve their payoff through unilaterally switching to a new strategy.

Vorobeychik and Wellman (2008) describe simulation-based games in terms of an oracle $\mathcal{O}$ that returns sample payoff observations such that, for any profile s, $\mathbb{E}[\mathcal{O}(s)] = u(s)$. In other words, a simulator can function as an oracle for some underlying game if the expected payoffs to each player in simulation are consistent with the payoff function $u(\cdot)$ for the game being simulated. The simulator may be noisy, necessitating repeated sampling to achieve accurate payoff estimates.

Figure 1 illustrates the basic EGTA procedure. Sets of heuristic strategies—one for each role—induce a space of profiles. We feed selected pure-strategy profiles to the game simulator, which outputs the observed payoff each agent received for playing its specified strategy in the profile. This output is used to update the payoff estimates for that profile in the empirical game model. At any point, we may choose to refine our game model by taking more samples of certain profiles, or adding more strategies and thus expanding the profile space, possibly using game-theoretic analysis of the current game model to inform these decisions. Once we have finished refining the empirical game model, we report the findings of our game-theoretic analysis.

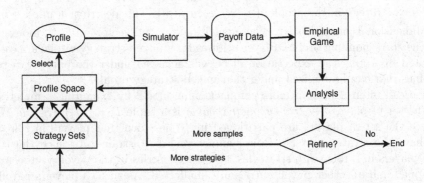

Fig. 1. Basic flow diagram of the iterative EGTA process

4   EGTAOnline

EGTAOnline is an experiment manager for simulation-based game studies. It provides researchers with distributed simulation scheduling and a robust data storage solution. Users of EGTAOnline can take advantage of the parallel and distributed computation afforded by a large cluster without having to learn the details of scheduling jobs onto the cluster. Users also benefit from a database management system for storing observation data without having to learn a database query language. As such, barriers to constructing large simulation-based games are dramatically reduced.

Figure 2 illustrates the role of EGTAOnline in the iterative EGTA process. The following subsections present the primary conceptual entities of EGTAOnline and how they support the construction of empirical games.

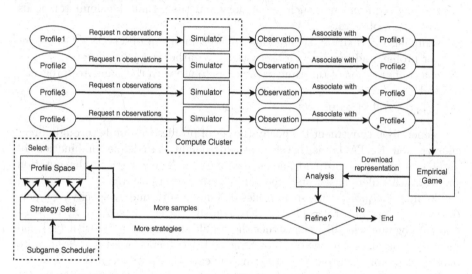

Fig. 2. Supporting the EGTA process with EGTAOnline

4.1   Simulators

To use EGTAOnline, researchers must write a *simulator program* that acts as an oracle, taking as input a pure-strategy profile s to sample, and outputting an *observation*. An observation must include a vector of payoffs and may include statistics about the simulation. This statistical information can be useful in statistical procedures, such as the use of control variates (Lavenberg and Welch, 1981) for reducing variance in payoff estimates. These statistics may also record variables that resulted from agent interaction, enabling analysis of the impact of strategic choices on non-payoff variables. The exchange of simulator input and output is conducted through a simple, file-based protocol, accommodating simulators developed with any programming language or simulation platform. A simulator program differs from the mathematical concept of a simulator described by Vorobeychik and Wellman (2008), as multiple simulators can be derived from a single simulator program through the specification of run-time parameters, or through specifying different assignments of players to roles. As such, a researcher can upload a single simulator program and perform multiple independent experiments.

4.2   Schedulers

Once a simulator program has been registered with EGTAOnline, the experimenter may create one or more *schedulers* for that simulator program. Schedulers translate user-specified requirements of the sampling process into simulation jobs that are scheduled onto a cluster. Specifically, schedulers take as input:

1. running requirements, such as memory and time, that the simulator needs to take an observation,
2. sampling information, such as maximum number of observations to gather per profile, and number of observations to gather per job request.
3. c, a configuration of run-time parameters to use with the simulator program, and
4. $\{s\}$, the collection of profiles to sample.

It is generally inconvenient to specify the set of profiles to sample through direct enumeration. EGTAOnline therefore provides facilities to define combinations of profiles generated according to a specified pattern. The current implementation supports schedulers based on three particularly useful patterns.

The first, *subgame*, generates profiles defining a subgame by specifying a partition of players into roles $\{I_j\}$, and restricted strategy sets $S'_j \subseteq S_j$ for each role j. Subgame schedulers construct the profile space associated with $\{I_j\}$ and $\{S'_j\}$ by generating the set of all symmetric assignments of strategies in S_j to players in I_j, for each role j, and taking the cartesian product of these sets.

The *deviation* pattern expands on a base set of profiles generated by a subgame scheduler by considering single-player deviations to alternative strategies. Users specify a partition of players into roles, and for each role j, two disjoint, restricted strategy sets: the base set S'_j and deviation set S''_j. The deviation scheduler uses the base sets $\{S'_j\}$ to generate profiles defining the full subgame over these strategies, as described above. To the subgame induced by $\{I_j\}$ and $\{S'_j\}$ are added any profiles that can be reached through one player switching to a strategy in its role's deviating strategy set, S''_j. This scheduler supports incrementally searching for payoff-improving strategy deviations, without constructing the exponentially larger subgame induced by adding these strategies to the base strategy sets.

The final scheduling pattern, *reduction*, generates profiles defining subgames (and optionally, deviations) for approximations based on reducing the effective number of players in the game. These approximations require exponentially fewer profiles than the corresponding full-player version of the game. EGTAOnline supports two types of reduction. In the *hierarchical* reduction (Wellman et al.,

2005), each player controls the strategy played by multiple agents in simulation of a corresponding full game profile. For example, we may approximate an 8-player symmetric game with a 4-player game in which each player specifies the strategy to be played by two agents in simulation. In the *deviation-preserving* reduction (Wiedenbeck and Wellman, 2012), each player controls one agent, but models the remaining players as proportionally controlling the remaining agents. This reduction is so named because it emphasizes preserving single-player deviation incentives—precisely those incentives which are important for establishing a Nash equilibrium—while still aggregating payoffs over many agents. Though profiles for either reduction scheduler are selected from a game with a reduced number of players, the profile objects that are stored in the database represent the assignment of strategies to agents in the unreduced game. For example, when a 2-player hierarchical reduction of a 4-player symmetric game requires a profile where one player, controlling two agents, plays strategy s_1 and the other player, also controlling two agents, plays strategy s_2, the profile that is requested of the simulator and stored in the database is (s_1, s_1, s_2, s_2). Consequently, observations gathered under a reduction scheduler may also be used in larger reduced game models, as well as in unreduced game models.

When constructing either reduction for games with multiple roles, each role may reduce the number of players at different rates. This feature can be useful when the strategy choices of players in a specific role have a greater impact on outcomes than the choices of players in other roles. If we were modeling the home buying market, for example, we may assume that changes in lending strategy by banks have a greater impact on outcomes than changes in the borrowing strategy adopted by individual home buyers, and thus want to approximate the banks' strategic choices more precisely than those of borrowers.

To enable arbitrary profile sampling behavior, EGTAOnline allows users to specify *generic schedulers*. Profiles to sample, and the number of samples requested, are passed to these schedulers through a JSON API. Users can write scripts with complex logic determining which profiles to sample, then send an HTTP request to update the scheduler accordingly. This feature, combined with the ability to request game representations through the JSON API, provides the flexibility necessary to support automated refinement of game models, discussed further in Section 6.

4.3 Simulations

A *simulation object* in EGTAOnline summarizes the state of a simulation job that has been scheduled on the cluster. A simulation job can request multiple observations be taken for a single profile, amortizing the overhead of scheduling on the cluster. Simulation objects record the current status of a job and any associated error messages. Errors can be caused by system problems, such as loss of network connectivity, failures in running the simulator, or any programmer-defined error. When a simulation returns with an error, the data gathered for that simulation is marked as invalid. Simulator programmers are encouraged to supply an informative error message whenever a state is reached that invalidates the observation data. This allows the user to detect and address error states that, while too rare to show up in preliminary testing, manifest themselves when many observations must be gathered.

4.4 Profiles

An EGTAOnline *profile object* associates a collection of *observation objects* with the pure-strategy profile, simulator program, and configuration of run-time parameters that generated those observations. An observation object stores payoff and feature data for each player in the associated profile, as well as any other statistics, that were recorded during a single run of the simulator. Distinguishing profile objects by simulator program and configuration enables consistent maintenance of observation data from many experiments. Different configurations of a simulator program correspond to different experimental setups, and as such, require separate profile object sets. Conversely, when a profile object already exists for a given simulator program, configuration, and strategy assignment, any new data is associated with that profile object. Thus, profiles can be in the sampling set of multiple schedulers, and associated with multiple games, allowing observational data to be included in all relevant analysis contexts—a topic we revisit in Section 5.

4.5 Games

A *game object* provides filtered views onto the current data. A game object defines a space of relevant profiles, based on a simulator program, configuration, partition of players into roles, and a strategy set for each role. When users request a representation of the game object, profile objects that match the specified criteria are collected and sent to the user in one of three available levels of detail. These profile objects carry with them all the associated observational data currently available, or summary statistics of the same.

5 Data Reuse

Gathering simulation data is a costly enterprise, particularly when many thousand different scenarios must be simulated, as in the construction of some empirical game models. As such, we would like to maximize the value of the previously gathered data through extensive reuse. Data reuse is a natural consequence of the iterative EGTA process (Figures 1 and 2), as game analysis and refinement decisions are made on an ever-expanding set of observations. This aspect of EGTA contrasts with many other applications of MABS. MABS studies typically observe fixed, but potentially adaptive, agent behavior in a particular simulated scenario. Although such studies may examine several different scenarios through a parameter sweep, the data from different scenarios are not analyzed together. Game-theoretic analysis, however, is based on comparing the outcomes of scenarios that differ by agent strategy selection.

Through the use of game objects, EGTAOnline makes it easy to compare observations in multiple game-theoretic contexts. EGTAOnline accomplishes this by defining what it means to be *comparable*—sharing the same partition of players into roles, simulator program, and configuration. Consider two game objects differing only in their strategy sets. By the definition provided above, the observations associated with these two game objects are comparable. Thus, if both game objects specify a single role with a strategy set that includes A, then observations of the profile where all players play A will be present in both game objects. Similarly, if we create a third game object that has as its strategy set the union of the strategies present in the first two game objects, it will contain all of the observations present in the other two game objects. Even though this larger game object subsumes the data from the other two, it is not always the preferred view of the data. Since most game analysis is super-linear in the number of profiles, game objects that restrict the strategy sets to only those currently under consideration take less time to assemble, download, and analyze.

As EGTAOnline provides a persistent data store, it is also easy to reexamine experiments long after they were originally conducted. If a new strategy is proposed for a particular scenario, testing whether it disrupts previous findings leverages all the previously gathered observations. Using a deviation scheduler, we can select profiles that correspond to unilateral deviations to the new strategy and determine whether such deviations refute previous equilibrium candidates. If the new strategy is a beneficial deviation, subsequent exploration still benefits from previously gathered observations as the profile space induced by adding this strategy to players' strategy sets contains the space of previously sampled profiles.

In previous work, we presented two procedures where such data reuse can be extremely valuable (Cassell and Wellman, 2012). We described an equilibrium search technique that iterates through increasingly fine-grained game reductions, establishing a restricted set of promising strategies in smaller game abstractions to reduce the space of profiles needed to identify equilibria in more fine-grained abstraction. Since reduced-game profiles are represented in EGTAOnline in terms of their unreduced game constituents, each iteration of this search benefits from the data gathered in previous steps. If we are applying this technique to a symmetric game with N players and are contemplating sampling the profiles of an n-player hierarchical reduction of this game, where n divides N, then for each positive integer n' that divides n, any profile in the n'-player hierarchical reduction corresponds to an unreduced game profile that has a counterpart in the n-player reduction, and thus observations of such profiles can be reused. As such, if all smaller reductions have already been explored, the number of previously unobserved profiles of the n-player reduction is given by the recursive relation

$$f(n, m) = \binom{n + m - 1}{m - 1} - \sum_{n' | n} f(n', m),$$

where m is the number of strategies.[1]

---

[1] Similar data reuse relationships can be constructed for role-symmetric hierarchical reductions and symmetric deviation preserving reductions.

Figure 3 demonstrates the fraction of profiles that are covered by smaller reductions, $\sum_{n'|n} f(n', m)/\binom{n+m-1}{m-1}$, for selected values of n and m. We can see that this fraction depends on the number of strategies as well as the divisors of n, but not explicitly on N, the number of players in the unreduced game. Consequently, when n is prime, this value decreases as n increases, whereas the relationship is non-monotonic for composite values of n. For small values of m, the prospect of performing another iteration of the equilibrium search with a more fine-grained reduction is much less daunting, since 40–60% of the space may have been explored in earlier steps. Furthermore, this level of data reuse between steps increases the likelihood that the equilibrium candidates identified in each step are close to those identified in previous steps.

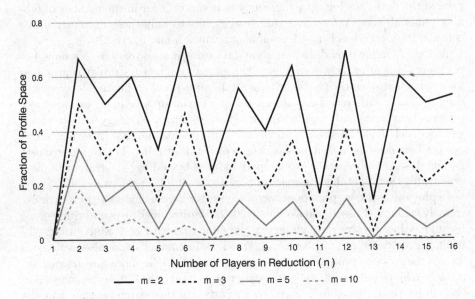

Fig. 3. Fraction of unreduced-game profile space for an n-player reduction that is covered by smaller reductions

A second task that benefits from convenient data reuse is the estimation of expectations of non-payoff variables. In this context, reuse takes the form of deriving multiple interpretations of data from a single empirical game model. We may wish to know, for example, which of several possible configurations of strategies lead to the highest expected price volatility in financial markets. When we restrict our attention to pure-strategy profiles, this task may be as simple as comparing the sample averages of the variable of interest for each profile under consideration. For mixed-strategy profiles, estimating the expectation of a non-payoff variable requires weighting our observations by the probability that the associated pure-strategy profile is realized under the specified mixed-strategy profile. For a game Γ and a distribution σ specifying the probability that each pure-strategy profile is played, we can estimate the conditional expectation of a non-payoff variable V under σ by

$$\mathbb{E}\left[V \mid \sigma\right] = \sum_{s \in \Gamma} \bar{V}_s \sigma(s),$$

where $\bar{V}_s$ is the sample average of V when simulating the pure-strategy profile s and $\sigma(s)$ is the probability that s is realized under σ. By storing the observations of V with the profile that was played during the observation, we can calculate and compare expectation estimates of V under different distributions of pure-strategy profile realizations without additional simulation. As with the addition of a new strategy, if a new solution concept is proposed, and thus different distributions over pure-strategy profiles are predicted, we can use all of our previously gathered observations in constructing the new estimate.

6   Automated Game Refinement

Typically, the game refinement step of the EGTA methodology requires human intervention. A researcher defines an experiment, performs the required simulation, and analyzes the resulting empirical game model. At this point, the researcher either reports findings or sets up another experiment, repeating the previous steps. In theory, these decisions could be made algorithmically, especially when future experiments are uniquely determined by the outcome of analysis. Practically though, interacting with EGTAOnline through submitting web forms is not optimized for computer-to-computer interaction.

To make automating the game refinement step simpler, EGTAOnline provides API access to its basic control functions. This API allows researchers to construct complex scripts that interact with EGTAOnline through HTTP requests. We describe two applications of automated game refinement and how they would be implemented with EGTAOnline.

6.1   Exploration of Profile Space

A common application of game-theoretic analysis is identifying Nash equilibria of a game. Though the problem of finding all Nash equilibria of an arbitrary game requires having observations of every profile, finding and validating a single equilibrium can often be accomplished through observations of a smaller space. Jordan et al. (2008) examined several algorithms to tackle the problem of exploring a game's profile space to quickly identify a Nash equilibrium. The authors treat identifying a Nash equilibrium as a search problem where each step identifies the next profile to sample. These algorithms are designed to sample profiles sequentially, focusing on identifying the *single best* profile to sample at any point in time. With EGTAOnline, several profiles may be sampled in parallel with little added cost. As such, extra information can be gathered in every step, and individual profile selection may be suboptimal.

One profile selection algorithm proposed by Jordan et al. is Minimum-Regret-First-Search (MRFS), which uses estimates of regret to guide search. The *regret* of a profile s, denoted $\epsilon(s)$, is the maximum improvement in payoff that a player can achieve through unilateral deviation. The key concept behind MRFS is that for every profile s, at any step in our search, we have a lower bound on the regret of s, $\hat{\epsilon}(s)$, defined to be the maximum payoff improvement thus far observed from evaluating profiles in $\mathcal{D}(s)$, the set of profiles that can be reached through a single player deviating from s. Once all profiles in $\mathcal{D}(s)$ have been evaluated, the value of $\epsilon(s)$ is *confirmed*. If the confirmed regret of a profile is zero, it is a Nash equilibrium.

At each step, MRFS chooses to sample a previously unobserved deviation from the profile s with the lowest unconfirmed regret bound. The profile to sample, $\bar{s}$, is chosen with the function SELECT-DEVIATION, which attempts to predict which profile is likely to provide the greatest benefit to the deviating player. After $\bar{s}$ has been sampled, the regret bounds of $\bar{s}$ and all profiles in $\mathcal{D}(\bar{s})$ are updated to reflect this new data.

Algorithm 1 presents a modification of MRFS to take advantage of parallel profile sampling. The Minimum-Regret-First-Search with Parallel Sampling (MRFSPS) schedules k profiles to be sampled in every step. It achieves this by replacing SELECT-DEVIATION with SELECT-MULTI-DEVIATIONS. When the profile s has more than k unobserved deviating profiles, the k deviating profiles most likely to increase $\hat{\epsilon}(s)$ are chosen for sampling. If the target profile s has no more than k unobserved deviating profiles, all deviating profiles are selected, and the profile with the next lowest unconfirmed regret is considered. The algorithm continues in this manner until k profiles have been selected for sampling, scheduling them to be sampled in parallel.

This algorithm is just one of several possible modifications to MRFS to take advantage of parallel sampling. Other algorithms discussed by Jordan et al. (2008), can also be modified to benefit from this capability. The comparison of these variants in terms of steps required to find a Nash equilibrium is left for future work.

6.2   Sequential Estimation of Empirical Games

Analyzing simulation-based games presents an added challenge over analytically specified games. Given the stochastic nature of simulation, how does one ensure that equilibria identified for an empirical game model are good approximations of equilibria of the game described by the simulator? Since EGTAOnline maintains the full history of observations and sampling decisions, we can pose the question of whether all deviations from a candidate equilibrium are statistically worse, to some level of significance. Posing the problem this way, validating a Nash equilibrium is a form of simulation optimization (Ólafsson and Kim, 2002), which

---

Algorithm 1. Minimum-Regret-First-Search with Parallel Sampling

---

Select first profile to sample at random, and add this profile to Queue
while Queue is not empty **do**
   $\ell \leftarrow \emptyset$
   $\mathcal{P} \leftarrow \emptyset$
   while $|\mathcal{P}| < k$ **and** ℓ does not contain all profiles in Queue **do**
      Select from Queue the lowest $\hat{\epsilon}(s)$ profile s not already in ℓ
      if s is confirmed **then**
         Remove s from Queue
         $\epsilon(s) \leftarrow \hat{\epsilon}(s)$
      else
         $\ell \leftarrow \ell \cup \{s\}$
         $\mathcal{P} \leftarrow \mathcal{P} \cup$ SELECT-MULTI-DEVIATIONS$(s, k - |\mathcal{P}|)$
      end if
   end while
   Sample all $\bar{s} \in \mathcal{P}$ in parallel
   for $\bar{s} \in \mathcal{P}$ **do**
      Insert $\bar{s}$ into Queue if previously unevaluated
      Update $\hat{\epsilon}(\hat{s})$ for $\hat{s} \in \{\bar{s}\} \cup \mathcal{D}(\bar{s})$ in Queue
   end for
end while

---

seeks to identify the best of several competing designs of a system or product through simulation. As such, we may appeal to the literature on optimal computing budget allocation (Chen and Lee, 2011), or the broader range of sequential estimation techniques (Ghosh et al., 1997), to decide how many additional samples of each profile to request at any decision point, as a function of statistical and strategic analysis of our accumulated game data. Figure 4 demonstrates how to conduct this sequential sampling procedure using EGTAOnline.

Confirming approximate Nash equilibria carries additional challenges not faced by more conventional sequential analysis problems. After gathering additional samples, payoff estimates for the game are updated, and thus equilibria candidates need to be recomputed. Vorobeychik (2010) demonstrates that regret in a simulation-based game almost surely converges to the regret in the underlying game as more observations are gathered, allaying concerns about the stability of the set of equilibria candidates. In other words, if an equilibrium candidate ceases to be a candidate after taking additional observations, then it is unlikely to be an equilibrium of the game that our simulator is modeling. Another challenge of using sequential techniques for this task is that our metric of interest, empirical regret, is unlikely to be well approximated by a simple distribution, constraining us to complicated, non-parametric procedures. To the best of our knowledge, the construction of optimal sequential sampling procedures for EGTA remains an open question.

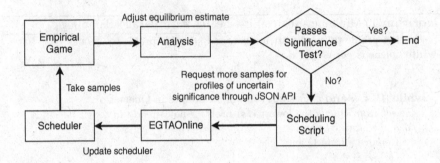

Fig. 4. Sequential sampling procedure to ensure statistical significance

7 In Production

We developed EGTAOnline to address a perceived need for robust sampling infrastructure to support the EGTA methodology. One way to assess if we have achieved our goal is to observe how the system is used by practitioners of the methodology, and how heavily they use the system. Though we are currently exploring options for sharing EGTAOnline, to this point users have been limited to our lab and some direct collaborators. Over the last seventeen months of use, approximately 8 million observations were recorded for 300,000 profiles. Many of these observations were generated for experiments detailed by Cassell and Wellman (2012), Wellman et al. (2012), and Dandekar et al. (2012). Our database currently has eleven distinct simulator programs registered, with multiple versions of some of these simulators. Schedulers (108) and games (95) significantly outnumber registered simulator programs (26), and have been used for exploring different simulator configurations and different profile spaces. Users are free to modify or delete schedulers and games, making these numbers significant underestimates of the number of the experiments that have been carried out thus far. There is considerable variety among the experiments conducted so far, ranging from explorations of the TAC Supply Chain Management game, where the simulation requires the parallel cooperation of multiple compute nodes, to an introduction-based routing protocol (Frazier et al., 2011), where role symmetry and hierarchical reduction are exploited. Though EGTAOnline in its current form has not been in use for very long, users are already taking advantage of its robust data storage system and high throughput.

8 Discussion

Creating large empirical game models through agent-based simulation carries many computational challenges. This does not mean, however, that we should not study large games. Many naturally occurring games, such as the stock market, are massive, and may be poorly modeled through analytical means or with small empirical game models. Though we have the raw computation to begin modeling and analyzing the strategic implications of these massive social systems, the lack of convenient tools can make significant exploration a daunting task.

EGTAOnline is part of an ongoing effort to provide the necessary software infrastructure to make constructing and analyzing large simulation-based games more commonplace. Though new features are planned, we have demonstrated that EGTAOnline already supports the complex simulation and analysis workflows necessary for the application of the EGTA methodology. EGTAOnline also makes substantial data reuse practical, limiting duplication of effort and supporting iterative approaches to game exploration and experimentation. Additionally, our system opens new avenues of research through support for parallel profile sampling and automated game refinement, setting the stage for the development of intelligent agents that manage the iterative process of scheduling profiles to be sampled and analyzing the results.

References

Alberts, S., Keenan, M.K., D'Souza, R.M.: Data-parallel techniques for simulating a mega-scale agent-based model of systemic inflammatory response syndrome on graphics processing units. Simulation 88(8), 895–907 (2012)

Bononi, L., Bracuto, M., D'Angelo, G., Donatiello, L.: Concurrent replication of parallel and distributed simulations. In: 19th Workshop on Principles of Advanced and Distributed Simulation, Monterey, CA, pp. 234–243 (2005)

Cassell, B.-A., Wellman, M.P.: Asset pricing under ambiguous information: An empirical game-theoretic analysis. Computational and Mathematical Organization Theory 18, 445–462 (2012)

Cassell, B.-A., Alperovich, T., Wellman, M.P., Noble, B.: Access point selection under emerging wireless technologies. In: Sixth Workshop on the Economics of Networks, Systems, and Computation, San Jose, CA (2011)

Chen, C.-H., Lee, L.H.: Stochastic Simulation Optimization: An Optimal Computing Budget Allocation. World Scientific Publishing Co., Singapore (2011)

Collins, J., Ketter, W., Pakanati, A.: An experiment management framework for TAC SCM agent evaluation. In: IJCAI 2009 Workshop on Trading Agent Design and Analysis, Pasadena, California, pp. 9–13 (2009)

Dandekar, P., Goel, A., Wellman, M.P., Wiedenbeck, B.: Strategic formation of credit networks. In: 21st International Conference on World Wide Web, Lyon, France (2012)

Frazier, G., Duong, Q., Wellman, M.P., Petersen, E.: Incentivizing responsible networking via introduction-based routing. In: McCune, J.M., Balacheff, B., Perrig, A., Sadeghi, A.-R., Sasse, A., Beres, Y. (eds.) Trust 2011. LNCS, vol. 6740, pp. 277–293. Springer, Heidelberg (2011)

Ghosh, M., Mukhopadhyay, N., Sen, P.K.: Sequential Estimation. John Wiley & Sons (1997)

Jordan, P.R., Kiekintveld, C., Wellman, M.P.: Empirical game-theoretic analysis of the TAC supply chain game. In: Sixth International Joint Conference on Autonomous Agents and Multiagent Systems, Honolulu, pp. 1188–1195 (2007)

Jordan, P.R., Vorobeychik, Y., Wellman, M.P.: Searching for approximate equilibria in empirical games. In: Seventh International Conference on Autonomous Agents and Multiagent Systems, Estoril, Portugal, pp. 1063–1070 (2008)

Lavenberg, S.S., Welch, P.D.: A perspective on the use of control variables to increase the efficiency of monte carlo simulations. Management Science 27(3), 322–335 (1981)

McKelvey, R.D., McLennan, A.M., Turocy, T.L.: Gambit: Software tools for game theory. Technical report, Version 0.2006.01.20 (2006), http://econweb.tamu.edu/gambit/

Mengistu, D., Davidsson, P., Lundberg, L.: Middleware support for performance improvement of MABS applications in the grid environment. In: Antunes, L., Paolucci, M., Norling, E. (eds.) MABS 2007. LNCS (LNAI), vol. 5003, pp. 20–35. Springer, Heidelberg (2008)

Nudelman, E., Wortman, J., Shoham, Y., Leyton-Brown, K.: Run the GAMUT: A comprehensive approach to evaluating game-theoretic algorithms. In: Third International Joint Conference on Autonomous Agents and Multiagent Systems, New York, pp. 880–887 (2004)

Ólafsson, S., Kim, J.: Simulation optimization. In: Winter Simulation Conference, San Diego, pp. 79–84 (2002)

Riley, P.F., Riley, G.F.: Spades: A distributed agent simulation environment with software-in-the-loop execution. In: 35th Winter Simulation Conference, New Orleans, pp. 817–825 (2003)

Sheutz, M., Harris, J.J.: An overview of the SimWorld agent-based grid experimentation system. In: Large-Scale Computing Techniques for Complex System Simulations. John Wiley & Sons (2012)

Vorobeychik, Y.: Probabilistic analysis of simulation-based games. ACM Transactions on Modeling and Computer Simulation 20(3) (2010)

Vorobeychik, Y., Wellman, M.P.: Stochastic search methods for Nash equilibrium approximation in simulation-based games. In: Seventh International Conference on Autonomous Agents and Multiagent Systems, Estoril, Portugal, pp. 1055–1062 (2008)

Wellman, M.P.: Methods for empirical game-theoretic analysis. In: 21st National Conference on Artificial Intelligence, Boston, pp. 1552–1555 (2006)

Wellman, M.P., Reeves, D.M., Lochner, K.M., Cheng, S.-F., Suri, R.: Approximate strategic reasoning through hierarchical reduction of large symmetric games. In: 20th National Conference on Artificial Intelligence, Pittsburgh, pp. 502–508 (2005)

Wellman, M.P., Sodomka, E., Greenwald, A.: Self-confirming price prediction strategies for simultaneous one-shot auctions. In: 28th Conference on Uncertainty in Artificial Intelligence, Catalina Island, CA (2012)

Wiedenbeck, B., Wellman, M.P.: Scaling simulation-based game analysis through deviation-preserving reduction. In: 11th International Conference on Autonomous Agents and Multiagent Systems, Valencia, pp. 931–938 (2012)

Agent-Based Modelling of Stock Markets Using Existing Order Book Data

Efstathios Panayi[1], Mark Harman[1], and Anne Wetherilt[2],*

[1] UCL, Gower Street, London WC1E 6BT, UK
[2] Bank of England, Threadneedle Street, London EC2R 8AH, UK

Abstract. We propose a new method for creating alternative scenarios for the evolution of a financial time series over short time periods. Using real order book data from the Chi-X exchange, along with a number of agents to interact with that data, we create a semi-synthetic time series of stock prices. We investigate the impact of using both simple, limited intelligence traders, along with a more realistic set of traders. We also test two different hypotheses about how real participants in the market would modify their orders in the alternative scenario created by the model. We run our experiments on 3 different stocks, evaluating a number of financial metrics for intra- and inter-day variability. Our results using realistic traders and relative pricing of real orders were found to outperform other approaches.

1 Introduction

The behaviour of stock prices over short horizons is an important consideration for both market participants and regulators, as the former need to be confident in their ability to place and execute their orders, while the latter need to ensure a smoothly functioning market. Currently, estimating the range of prices that could arise in the short term is predominantly focused on analysing past data and fitting statistical models to specific time series from which they come. This approach is based on the assumption that past market conditions are likely to be repeated at some point in the future. However, it is very restrictive, as it does not allow for scenarios that have not previously occurred [23], or have occurred only very rarely (such as large, rapid intra-day movements). Unfortunately, this restriction is highly problematic, because such infrequent, rapid intra-day movements denote one of the largest market risks.

Agent-based modelling is a well established method for creating alternative scenarios in a financial market, the first work on this being conducted 3 decades ago [6]. The agent-based approach seeks to program the behaviour of individual traders, and their interaction gives rise to changes in the intra-day behaviour of orders and prices. Agent-based modelling offers many more parameters that can be altered to generate different scenarios. It also facilitates the study of emergent properties of traders' interactions and particular classes of traders in isolation.

---

* The views expressed in this paper are the authors' and are not necessarily those of the Bank of England.

F. Giardini and F. Amblard (Eds.): MABS 2012, LNAI 7838, pp. 101–114, 2013.
© Springer-Verlag Berlin Heidelberg 2013

Agent-based modelling has, so far, been used primarily for stock market simulation with a focus on longer time frames than intra-day behaviour. A key challenge for agent-based models is to demonstrate that the resulting price dynamics are indeed consistent with known empirical facts. Such 'stylised facts' may include volatility clustering and 'fat tails' in distributions of financial returns (Engle and Russell [21]).

In this paper, we seek to combine realistic data and an agent-based model to achieve a simulation that exploits real world data. We start with 3 high quality data sets from the Chi-X exchange and rebuild the order book so that we can pause the market at any time and examine the bids and offers for the stock, along with any order executions and cancellations. We then add different classes of agents to interact with this 'live' order book, so that the evolution of the stock price is modified by the interaction with our agents.

In particular, in this paper we introduce and empirically compare a class of almost zero-intelligence traders, along with a class of traders that is based on more realistic behaviour and compare their impact on the stock price. We also experiment and report on two different ways of incorporating real data into the model: absolute and relative pricing. The former assumes that if traders in the real market were participating in the synthetic market, they would have submitted their orders at exactly the same prices they had originally. The latter method assumes that traders would have shifted the price of their orders by the difference between the stock price in the synthetic market and in the real market.

We empirically evaluate the behaviour of the stock price resulting from the model for 3 of the most frequently traded stocks on the Chi-X exchange (Arcelor Mittal, Deutsche Bank and GDF Suez). We do this by comparing the ranges of maximum, minimum and closing prices produced by multiple runs of the model, and running tests for fat tails and volatility clustering of the returns distribution.

This paper contributes to the existing literature on agent-based modelling of financial markets in two ways: Firstly, it introduces the concept of semi-synthetic modelling, which combines past data and agents in a single simulation, and intuitively should be closer to the real market than a pure agent-based model. Secondly, whereas existing studies have longer horizons, we focus on short-term behaviour of stock prices and study the returns at the transaction level. Our interest in short-term market behaviour is motivated by the rapid intra-day drop and recovery in the US equities market, during the May 6, 2010 'Flash Crash', which created concerns about short term prioprietary trading behaviour [12].

The rest of this paper is organised as follows: Section 2 introduces the experimental framework employed in this study and describes the two classes of traders that we compare, along with the two ways of handling the real order book data. Section 3 presents the research questions and gives some detail about the stocks we study. Section 4 then presents the results of batch runs of our model. Section 5 suggests potential weaknesses of our study. Section 6 summarises related work in the area of agent-based modelling of markets. Section 7 concludes.

2   Agent-Based Simulation with ORder Book Data (ABSORBD)

Our model aims to replicate the activity of a single day on the Chi-X exchange. The two main types of orders are market orders, where a trader can buy or sell a particular amount of stock at the best price available at the moment, or a limit order, where the trader specifies a price above which she is unwilling to buy, if she submits a bid, or a price under which she is unwilling to sell, if she submits an offer for a stock. If a limit order isn't executed immediately in its entirety, it enters the order book, where bids and offers are prioritised by price, then by time, in the case of tie breaks.

2.1   Stylised Facts

In agent-based models of financial markets, it is standard practice to measure the validity of the model by investigating whether the stock price exhibits particular characteristics, known as the 'stylised facts'. There are a number of ways to replicate these characteristics, a summary of which is presented in Section 6.

While the literature about stylised facts, which commenced with Mandelbrot [17], was initially concerned with characteristics of markets at longer time scales, Engle and Russell [21] demonstrated that these characteristics also apply to the intra-day level. This paper studies the behaviour of prices at a very high frequency, namely the change in price between two subsequent transactions. We evaluate our model based on the following two widely used stylised facts, also illustrated in Figure 1:

1. Fat tails. This means that, when plotting the distribution of returns of the financial asset, the probability of very high or very low returns is higher than that implied by a normal distribution with the same mean and standard deviation. The degree of 'fat-tailedness' is called kurtosis, and is the fourth moment of the distribution. The normal distribution has a kurtosis of 3, and a distribution with a kurtosis above 3 is called leptokurtic, or fat-tailed.
2. Volatility clustering. This means that a large change in the asset price (over a minute, for example) is more likely to be followed by a large change, and the same is true for small changes in the asset price. The time series for which this is true are called 'heteroscedastic' (i.e. of differing variability), and we can test whether a series is heteroscedastic with the Engle ARCH-LM test.

2.2   Synthetic Trader Behaviour

In our model, we create alternative scenarios for the evolution of a stock price over a day by recreating the order book for a single stock with real orders and then adding synthetic traders who also submit orders. We investigate the impact of agent behaviour on the stock price and other market characteristics, described in 2.1. In particular, we implement 2 different classes of synthetic traders and compare their impact on the market.

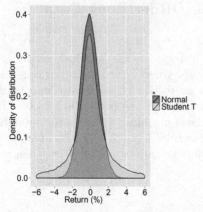

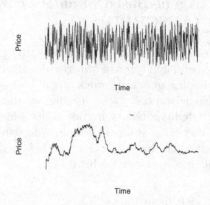

Normal and Student T distributions. Note the shorter middle and fatter tails of the Student T distribution.

Homoscedastic and heteroscedastic time series. The variability is constant in the upper (homoscedastic) time series, but changes in the lower (heteroscedastic) plot.

Fig. 1. Fat-tails and volatility clustering, two of the most common characteristics of financial time series

Our first class of traders consists of homogeneous 'Limited Intelligence' (LI) traders, similar to those proposed by LiCalizi and Pelizzari [15] and in the physics literature, for example by Maslov [18]. LI traders' decisions are unaffected by the stock price and only take into account their budget constraints when determining whether to submit a trade. We call these limited, as opposed to zero intelligence traders, as they don't place orders at prices that are worse than are available in the prevailing market and they stop when they have reached their cash limit. Although their trading behaviour would not arise from any meaningful strategy, is useful to implement as a baseline against which to compare it to other behaviours.

In our model, LI traders become active after a certain amount of trading activity in the market, which varies for each trader. When a particular trader becomes active, she decides whether to submit a bid or an offer for the stock, with X% and (100-X)% probability respectively. If she is still within her budget, she continues with her order and detemines the price and size randomly: The order price is uniformly distributed in the range of Y% below or above the best bid or offer respectively, while the size (in shares) is uniformly distributed within the limits [1,Z].

Our second class of traders is based on more realistic trader behaviour. Kirilenko et al. [12] study the composition of the E-mini S&P 500 stock index futures market, and identify 6 major categories of market participants:

1. Intermediaries, who usually post prices on both sides of the order book and try to maintain their position throughout the day, making their income from the difference between their bid and offer prices.
2. High Frequency Traders, who have a relatively low net position throughout the day, compared to their activity. They are similar to intermediaries, but have much higher trading activity and much shorter holding periods.
3. Fundamental Buyers, who try to build a long position during the day.
4. Fundamental Sellers, who try to build a short position during the day.
5. Opportunistic Traders, who may behave as intermediaries at times, or as fundamental traders at times when they see significant directional moves.
6. Small Traders, who show very limited trading activity.

We implement all of these categories (except the Small Traders, who have very little, if any, effect on the stock price) in our second class and will refer to the traders as Kirilenko (KI) traders collectively. Our first class comprises 1000 LI traders. Our second class consists of 394 KI traders, distributed as shown in in Table 1. These numbers were chosen based on the classification in [12] and to produce the empirical features in 2.1.

Table 1. Trader Information

Trader type	Number
Intermediary	40
HFT	4
Opportunistic	150
Fundamental Buyer	100
Fundamental Seller	100

2.3   Handling of Real Order Book Data

As we are adding synthetic traders to interact with our full order book data from the Chi-X exchange, we have to make some assumptions about how the real traders would have reacted to the modified stock prices. As the order book only provides anonymous trading data, we cannot identify individual trading strategies, and hence we need to make assumptions as to how they would have interacted with either LI or KI traders.

To do so, we consider two approaches. For our first method (referred to as the absolute pricing method), we assume that if the 'real' traders (i.e. the traders that submitted the orders in our dataset) were participants in our synthetic market, they would have submitted their orders at exactly the same price, independently of what happened to the stock price during the day. Then, in our hybrid model, real traders recreate the historical environment by repeating their original actions, and their decisions are unaffected by the additional trading activity of the synthetic agents.

The second method (labelled the relative pricing method) assumes that traders submit orders with prices that are relative to the prevailing stock price. So if the price in the synthetic stock market is higher, the orders read in from the real dataset will also be higher by the same relative amount. With this configuration, even traders from the original dataset become reactive, albeit in an unsophisticated way. This is perhaps a more realistic assumption about how market participants would react to seeing different stock prices.

3   Experimental Setup

As we are creating a semi-synthetic model, it seems reasonable to aim for a market where approximately half of the trades come from the real dataset, with the other half coming from our synthetic market participants. Since this precise split cannot be achieved in every run, we allow for runs where the number of trades in which at least one of the traders is synthetic is at least 30%. We adjust the number of traders and frequency with which they visit the market, in order to achieve this split.

3.1   Dataset Description

This paper uses full order book data for 3 stocks from the Chi-X exchange on 3/1/2011, for which some detail is presented in Figure 2 and Table 2. These datasets are very detailed and contain every order to buy or sell a stock that was submitted to the exchange, the size of those orders, the time of submission and any executions or cancellations.

Table 2. Company information about the 3 stocks in our study

Company	Value(bil.)
GDF Suez	59
Arcelor Mittal	44
Deutsche Bank	35

3.2   Research Questions

In order to study the validity of our semi-synthetic model, we measure the impact on 5 inter- and intra-day variability measures:

- Closing, maximum and minimum prices observed over the day
- Kurtosis and volatility clustering.

These metrics are then used in our research questions, in order to investigate the impact of our design choices. These are as follows:

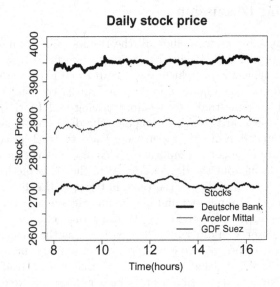

Fig. 2. The evolution of the stock prices for the 3 companies studied (on 3/1/2011)

1. What is the effect on the market metrics mentioned above, of using absolute and relative pricing?
2. What is the effect on the market metrics mentioned above, of using simple (LI) and realistic (KI) traders?

In particular, for the first 3 metrics, we use a separate dataset of 60 points of coarse-grained (daily) data around our trading day from Yahoo! Finance, in order to construct boxplots of the difference between the closing, maximum and minimum prices and the starting price of the day. We then produce similar boxplots from 60 simulation runs for each design choice and compare the results of each batch run.

In more detail, the summary output of the coarse-grained, real dataset is compared to the summary outputs of separate batch runs where we use:

1. Absolute pricing and LI traders
2. Relative pricing and LI traders
3. Absolute pricing and KI traders
4. Relative pricing and KI traders

To measure volatility clustering, we use the Engle ARCH-LM test for conditional heterscedasticity, whose null hypothesis is that a particular return distribution exhibits no ARCH effects(i.e. volatility is constant throughout the day). We study which of the four options mentioned above will produce runs in which this null hypothesis is rejected (and thus, there is clustering of volatility).

4   Results and Discussion

As space does not allow us to include all the results of our simulation, Table 3 and the boxplots in Figure 4 give us summary information, while Figure 3 demonstrates four typical runs, which allow us to zoom in on the data. We see that in the second graph of Figure 3, we have an almost constant upward trend and we find that all runs that use absolute pricing and LI traders result in either upward or downward trends throughout the day. This is because of the homogeneous construction of the traders, and leads to stock price moves that are similar in nature (but not in amplitude). This also means that the volatility is more constant throughout the day, compared to the other methods.

Figure 4 shows the variability of the runs, in terms of the difference between the starting and closing, minimum and maximum prices of the day. We see that using absolute pricing greatly constrains the range of maximum, minimum and closing prices we observe in our runs, whereas it seems that using either LI or KI traders and relative pricing produces results that are reasonably close to the range of real prices. We see that our batch runs that use KI traders, however, produce daily maxima that are significantly higher than that we observe in the real dataset. So the combination of relative pricing and KI traders must give rise to higher intra-day volatility, something which we confirm by looking at the individual runs.

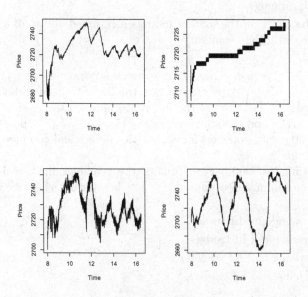

Fig. 3. Four sample stock runs, using absolute or relative pricing and LI traders(top) and absolute or relative pricing and KI traders(bottom)

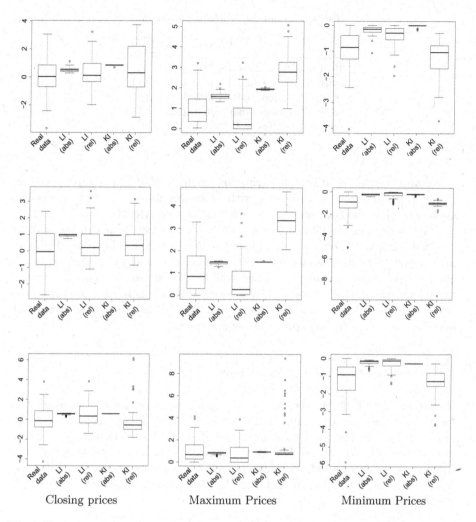

Fig. 4. Variation of the percentage difference between starting prices and closing, maximum and minimum prices observed in real data and in runs of our semi-synthetic model for GDF Suez(top), Arcelor Mittal(middle) and Deutsche Bank(bottom)

Next, investigate the two market characteristics often observed in the real markets, namely fat tails and volatility clustering. The distribution of returns from our model has fatter tails than the normal distribution, as the kurtosis is much higher than 3, using either LI or KI traders, and under either absolute or relative pricing. The relative order book pricing/KI traders combination, however, produces time series with higher kurtosis, as we can see in Table 3. We have already noted that this combination produces a more volatile stock price, and the aggressive nature of some of the traders also causes price jumps, and thus higher kurtosis.

Table 3. Summary kurtosis information

	GSZp	MTa	DBKd
Real Order book data	29.0	10.1	8.8
with LI traders (abs)	45.2	13.0	35.1
with LI traders (rel)	43.5	13.0	43.5
with KI traders (abs)	36.9	15.3	32.3
with KI traders (rel)	81.3	152	99.7

We also test for volatility clustering, using the ARCH-LM test proposed by Engle [10]. For 3 of the 4 options, with high probability, the test rejects the hypothesis that the time series of returns exhibits no ARCH effects. Therefore, the time series must exhibit differing volatility at various points in the trading day, which is what we observe in real markets also. For the combination of relative pricing and LI traders, however, we have some runs in which the hypothesis is not rejected, which means there is no sufficient evidence that volatility varies throughout the day. We have already mentioned that this result comes from the homogeneous construction of LI traders, and the end result is a time series that doesn't meet the volatility clustering requirement.

4.1   Answers to Research Questions

Regarding the effect of absolute pricing, our results indicate that using this assumption for the behaviour of traders in the real dataset produces a very narrow range of prices and thus cannot be used in a model that aims to create alternative scenarios for the short-term behaviour of a stock price. Using relative pricing, on the other hand, allows the price in the simulated market to drift away from the price in the real market and thus the model can create a reasonable range of prices.

Regarding the effect of simple (LI) traders, their homogeneity is problematic, as although batch runs (with relative pricing) produce reasonable ranges of prices, we also see unrealistic stock price behaviour, with constant upward or downward trends. In addition, the time series of stock prices in many simulation runs fails the volatility clustering requirement that we need to show similarity to real financial time series. Using realistic (KI) traders with relative pricing produces reasonable ranges again, but also meets the volatility clustering requirement. While the price ranges do not match up exactly with the ranges produced from the real dataset (particularly with regards to the maximum prices observed in the day), our results demonstrate that of the four combinations tested, relative pricing with KI traders produces simulation runs that are closest to real financial time series overall, taking into account the range of prices produced in the simulation, as well as the presence of fat tails in the returns distribution and of volatility clustering in the prices.

5   Limitations and Threats to Validity

The categories of traders mentioned in Kirilenko et al. [12] provide only a high level description of the strategies followed. As such, there is a degree of flexibility in implementing these strategies for our synthetic agents and we have had to select what we believe are sensible values for a number of parameters.

In addition, we have only tested the semi-synthetic model on the intra-day stock prices of 3 companies. Also, our dataset only covered a single trading day, and both these factors limit the degree to which we can generalise our results.

6   Related Work

Research regarding the simulation of financial markets using agent-based modelling can be traced back 30 years ago to the work of Cohen et al. [6], who proposed a model for a stock exchange. Cohen evaluated the impact of various stabilising policies on price, volatility and liquidity. He also introduced the concept of heterogeneous trading agents and an architecture for the limit order book, ideas which have been replicated in many forms since.

More recently, a variety of approaches have been suggested, each drawing from a wide and varied literature, including Finance, Economics, Mathematics, Statistics and Physics. The aims of these approaches vary, from trying to implement 'rational' models of trader behaviour to reproducing particular statistical features of markets. More details can be found in the surveys of LeBaron [13] and Chakraborti et al. [2]. Cristelli et al. [8] studied the commonalities, strengths and deficiencies of existing models and proposed additional questions to be considered in future models.

The Santa Fe Artificial Stock Market ([19,1,14]), is one of the best-known examples of agent-based financial markets. Santa Fe agents make trading decisions based on binary market descriptors, and their strategies evolve in order to maximize profitability. The papers above also deal with the rate of evolution of the strategies, and how this gives rise to different regimes; the rational expectations regime and a more complex regime, where bubbles and crashes may appear. Other evolutionary approaches can be found in Chen and Yeh [4], Lux and Schornstein [16] and Pereira et al. [20].

Another strand of research in the agent-based modelling of financial markets literature attempts to recreate market characteristics by giving agents more realistic strategies, similar to the second class of traders implemented in this paper. This was initially attempted by Kim and Markowitz [11] and has been studied more recently by Westerhoff and Reitz [22] and Chiarella and Iori [5].

In this literature, a model is generally validated by showing that the time series of asset prices it produces exhibits certain stylised facts, or common characteristics of financial markets [14,5,16]. In this paper, we examined fat tails in the distribution of returns and volatility clustering, which are the properties that the vast majority of agent-based models try to explain through their specification [3]. A review of these stylised facts can be found in Cont [7], while Chen [3] identifies a total of 30 of these statistical properties of financial time series that are replicated through agent-based models.

7   Conclusions

In this paper we have introduced semi-synthetic agent-based modelling, a new concept in the area of agent-based modelling of financial markets. Intuitively, a model for a stock market that is partially based on real order book data and partially based on agents should be closer to the real market than a pure agent-based model, in terms of simulated price dynamics. Our tests generate realistic runs of daily trading, when assuming that traders from the real markets (i.e. the traders that had submitted the orders in the real dataset) would have submitted their orders to buy or sell stocks not as suggested in the dataset, but shifted by the difference between the price they see in the simulated market and the price they had seen on the real market. If, in contrast, traders would have submitted their orders at exactly the same price, simulations that use both simple and realistic trading agents to interact with the real orders yield price dynamics which closely mimic those observed during the actual trading day, which is not useful when seeking to investigate alternative possible scenarios.

We investigated the effect of using homogeneous, limited intelligence traders compared to more varied, realistic traders, for the synthetic part of our model. Using realistic traders gave us the closest match with real markets, in terms of the market characteristics we measured. Using almost random traders gave us good results with regards to the range of prices achieved, but studying individual runs showed that the homogeneity of these traders gives rise to price behaviour not normally associated with intra-day price dynamics (constant upward or downward trends, as well as atypical volatility).

We believe that these results are promising, as they show that from a limited dataset (one trading day, in particular), we can generate thousands of realistic alternative scenarios. We hope that by extending this research, it will be possible to identify potential problems, like intra-day booms and crashes, and consider the impact from a range of policy measures.

In the future, we plan to evaluate methods for parameter selection for the synthetic agents in our model. Our goal is to produce realistic alternative trading scenarios, so our objectives will include matching particular moments in the simulated and real time series. The simulated method of moments has already been used for this purpose, but as we plan to evaluate multiple objectives, we believe multi-objective evolutionary algorithms, such as NSGA-II [9], would also be promising methods for parameter selection.

Future work will extend our results by using datasets with more companies and multiple trading days, in order to provide a more complete picture of the behaviour of our model. In particular, we are interested in studying the effect of the dynamics of the underlying trading day on the time series that results from the hybrid model.

References

1. Arthur, W.B., Holland, J.H., LeBaron, B.D., Palmer, R.G., Tayler, P.: Asset Pricing Under Endogenous Expectations in an Artificial Stock Market. SSRN eLibrary (1996)
2. Chakraborti, A., Muni Toke, I., Patriarca, M., Abergel, F.: Econophysics: Empirical facts and agent-based models. ArXiv e-prints (September 2009)
3. Chen, S.H., Chang, C.I., Du, Y.R.: Agent-based economic models and econometrics. The Knowledge Engineering Review, 1–46 (2009)
4. Chen, S.H., Yeh, C.H.: Evolving traders and the business school with genetic programming: A new architecture of the agent-based artificial stock market. Journal of Economic Dynamics and Control 25(3-4), 363–393 (2001)
5. Chiarella, C., Iori, G.: A simulation analysis of the microstructure of double auction markets. Quantitative Finance 2(5), 346–353 (2002)
6. Cohen, K.J., Maier, S.F., Schwartz, R.A., Whitcomb, D.K.: A simulation model of stock exchange trading. Simulation 41(5), 181–191 (1983)
7. Cont, R.: Empirical properties of asset returns: stylized facts and statistical issues. Quantitative Finance 1(2), 223–236 (2001)
8. Cristelli, M., Pietronero, L., Zaccaria, A.: Critical Overview of Agent-Based Models for Economics. ArXiv e-prints (January 2011)
9. Deb, K., Pratap, A., Agarwal, S., Meyarivan, T.: A fast elitist multi-objective genetic algorithm: Nsga-ii. IEEE Transactions on Evolutionary Computation 6, 182–197 (2000)
10. Engle, R.F.: A general approach to lagrange multiplier model diagnostics. Journal of Econometrics 20(1), 83–104 (1982)
11. Kim, G., Markowitz, H.: Investment Rules, Margin, and Market Volatility. Journal of Portfolio Management 16(1), 45–52 (1989)
12. Kirilenko, A.A., Kyle, A.P., Samadi, M., Tuzun, T.: The Flash Crash: The Impact of High Frequency Trading on an Electronic Market. Social Science Research Network Working Paper Series (October 2010), http://ssrn.com/abstract=1686004
13. LeBaron, B.: Agent-based computational finance: Suggested readings and early research. Journal of Economic Dynamics and Control 24(5-7), 679–702 (2000)
14. LeBaron, B., Arthur, W., Palmer, R.: Time series properties of an artificial stock market. Journal of Economic Dynamics and Control 23(9-10), 1487–1516 (1999)
15. Licalzi, M., Pellizzari, P.: Fundamentalists clashing over the book: a study of order-driven stock markets. Quantitative Finance 3(6), 470–480 (2003)
16. Lux, T., Schornstein, S.: Genetic learning as an explanation of stylized facts of foreign exchange markets. Journal of Mathematical Economics 41(1-2), 169–196 (2005)
17. Mandelbrot, B.: The Variation of Certain Speculative Prices. The Journal of Business 36(4), 394–419 (1963)
18. Maslov, S.: Simple model of a limit order-driven market. Physica A: Statistical Mechanics and its Applications 278(3-4), 571–578 (2000)
19. Palmer, R., Arthur, W.B., Holland, J.H., LeBaron, B., Tayler, P.: Artificial economic life: a simple model of a stockmarket. Physica D: Nonlinear Phenomena 75(1-3), 264–274 (1994)
20. da Costa Pereira, C., Mauri, A., Tettamanzi, A.G.B.: Cognitive-agent-based modeling of a financial market. In: Proceedings of the 2009 IEEE/WIC/ACM International Joint Conference on Web Intelligence and Intelligent Agent Technology, WI-IAT 2009, vol. 2, pp. 20–27. IEEE Computer Society, Washington, DC (2009)

21. Russell, J.R., Engle, R.F.: Analysis of high-frequency data. In: Aït-Sahàlia, Y., Hansen, L.P. (eds.) Handbook of Financial Econometrics, pp. 383–426. North-Holland, San Diego (2010)
22. Westerhoff, F., Reitz, S.: Nonlinearities and cyclical behavior: The role of chartists and fundamentalists. Studies in Nonlinear Dynamics & Econometrics 7(4), 3 (2003)
23. Zigrand, J.P., Shin, H.S., Beunza, D.: Feedback effects and changes in the diversity of trading strategies. The future of Computer Trading in Financial Markets (2011), http://www.bis.gov.uk/assets/bispartners/foresight/docs/computer-trading/11-1221-dr2-feedback-effects-and-changes-in-diversity-of-trading-strategies.pdf

Parallel Execution of Social Simulation Models in a Grid Environment

Davide Nunes and Luis Antunes

GUESS/LabMAg/Universidade de Lisboa, Portugal
{davide.nunes,xarax}@di.fc.ul.pt

Abstract. The exploration of agent-based social simulation models with a systematic analysis over its parameter space leads to a common problem. It takes too much time to get enough results for a significant analysis of the data generated by the simulation runs over those models. In this paper we show how one can minimise this problem by using grid computing. That is, constructing a social simulation model, designing an experiment and distributing the experiment over a computer grid, running a social simulation model with different parameter combinations in parallel. We supply a working example using the MASON framework and the JPPF framework.

Keywords: agent-based, social simulation, grid computing, experiment exploration, social simulation tools.

1 Introduction

In the exploration of social simulation models we encounter a common problem which is deeply related to the analysis of the effects of different parameter combinations. The problem is that if a model parameter space is big enough, running simulations over that space is very demanding and takes a huge amount of time. The models are often executed on a single machine and the runs are executed sequentially. We can have a machine with multiple cores but the parallel execution of the simulations over the models is restricted to the number of the cores a processor has. We intend to show how one can eliminate such a problem by setting up a simple computer grid using multiple machines.

In this case, a grid is simply a set of networked loosely coupled computers acting together to perform very large tasks [14].

Considering a single machine as a processing unit, it is easy to see that more processing units can reduce the time necessary to run through the parameter space of a social simulation experiment. As an example, if one has ten processing units available in the grid, these can be used to process ten simulations over a model in the same time it would take to run a single simulation in a single processing unit, roughly in one tenth of the time. We say roughly because the performance gain is not linear [17]. This is specially true when we deal with grid systems as we will discuss later. The benefits of using a grid system are clearly expressed in [19].

F. Giardini and F. Amblard (Eds.): MABS 2012, LNAI 7838, pp. 115–129, 2013.
© Springer-Verlag Berlin Heidelberg 2013

We want show how it is possible to reduce the time taken in the exploration of the simulation parameter space by executing different parameter configurations in parallel using a computer grid.

When we have models that encompass a multiplicity of parameters, we want to explore them and analyse the results over the possible combinations of the parameter values. For simple models, the problem does not reside in the time consumed in the execution of a simulation run, but rather in the time consumed on the exploration of sometimes huge parameter spaces. Tools like NetLogo [20] allow for the execution of multiple runs in a single machine but, like described before, this is limited by the number of cores a machine possesses. Other tools like MASON [11] are more efficient than NetLogo. In this case, MASON is optimized for running in a single thread efficiently, using one core of a machine (we can however run multiple simulations in multiple threads just like in NetLogo).

The purpose of this paper is to identify a simple way to exploit a grid system for agent-based simulation models without the need for a deep understanding of grid computing. We present a simple implementation using the discrete-event agent-based framework MASON [11] and JPPF (Java Parallel Processing Framework) [5]. We chose MASON as this is a very simple platform to develop agent-based models in Java, yet, out-of-the-shelf examples of simulation models deployed in grid systems, are not available for this framework.

The paper is organised as follows. In section 2, we describe available implementations of agent-based simulation models coupled with grid systems. Although not within the scope of this work, we also discuss some approaches on parameter space exploration and agent-based simulation optimisation. Section 3 offers both a simple formal and informal explanation on how the simulation experiments are distributed using a grid environment. In this section we then discuss the expected speedup enhancements from the parallel exploration of simulation experiments. We also show empirical results for the distribution of simple tasks in a small grid, allowing the reader to visualise the discussed concepts within a real scenario. Finally, in section 4, we present some details about the concrete implementation presented in this paper. We wrap up with some conclusions and supply some additional resources for the described implementation.

2   Related Work

This section describes some of the related work regarding the usage of grid computing to execute agent-based simulation models as well as some aspects of parameter space exploration.

In this paper we provide and discuss a simple implementation for agent-based simulation experiment distribution in a grid environment, using the MASON framework [11], similar work exist for other platforms. For Repast [6] for instance, some efforts have been made to provide some grid computing templates. Examples of such efforts are the work of Chen et al. [4] and Gulyas et al. [9]. In the first approach, simulation components are distributed in a grid through the usage of a High-Level Architecture Grid (HLA-Grid). In this approach, simulation components, such as agents or environments, are decoupled and processed within the grid system. The work in [9] describes an effort to conceive different templates for distributed agent-based simulations. The templates are not running models executed within a grid system, but rather different methods to distribute the simulation models themselves, similarly to what is done in [4]. Nevertheless, this work provides interesting insights on complex systems simulation on the grid, as well as simulation partitioning.

Alternative ways to distribute simulation models comprehend for instance the usage of platforms where agents are intrinsically distributed. Examples of such platforms are for instance JADE [2] or ZASE [21].

Another interesting related subject is on how to design agent-based experiments and how to organise and explore the simulation parameter space. Regarding parameter space exploration, in [18], Terano deals with huge parameter spaces from a social simulation point of view. This work presents an inverse simulation approach to deal with model parameter definition. Instead of designing the simulation experiments with a starting set of parameters and consequently analysing the simulation results, a target global function defining a desired outcome is used to find the necessary initial parameters for the intended result. A similar approach is explored by Stonedah in [16]. These two approaches ([18,16]) are exactly the opposite from the simulation approach presented in this paper but present interesting insights on alternative ways to explore parameter spaces.

Finally, although in this paper we present performance results for the grid system being used in our implementation, these are empirical and used as complementary to the understanding of grid environments without dwelling much on technical details. Regarding the performance of multi-agent simulation models in grid systems, the work in [13,12] describes a way to support efficient execution of large-scale multi-agent-based systems on a Grid environment. This is done either by performance prediction, in the case of [13], where a model of agent-based application performance is developed, or performance optimisation [12], where a simulation model based on JADE [2] is optimised in terms of agent placement within the system distributed nodes.

3 Parallel Exploration of the Parameter Space

In this section we describe how we can explore parameter spaces using a computer grid. We start by presenting an informal overview over the parallel exploration process and then formalize the concepts presented. Finally we present a comprehensive empirical analysis of the performance gains one can get from the usage of a grid system to execute social simulation experiments.

3.1 Parallel Exploration Process Overview

A grid of computers executes working units called Jobs. Jobs have multiple independent tasks that can be executed separately. The job tasks can then be executed in parallel, by assigning them to different machines in the grid for execution.

So, we have to create agent-based model instances as tasks and create jobs by coupling multiple model instances (tasks). The next step is to submit the jobs to the grid and wait for results. Sending a job to the grid will distribute the execution of the tasks (the model instances) across the available grid machines. All of this is made using the JPPF framework and we discuss it latter when dealing with the working example.

We can explain the parallel exploration process informally as follows (see figure 1):

1. identify the social simulation experiment parameter space P (set of parameters considered and the respective domain for each parameter);
2. take the parameter space and divide it into c unique configurations in which a configuration is a set of parameter values (one value for each parameter);
3. construct grid jobs with r tasks. Each task is a configured agent-based model in which the model parameter values are drawn from the parameter space configurations. We consider the same configuration for one job, r is then the number of runs to be executed for each parameter configuration;
4. submit the jobs to the grid.
5. collect the results of the different simulation runs. The grid should be considered as a black box where we submit jobs and collect results when these are available;

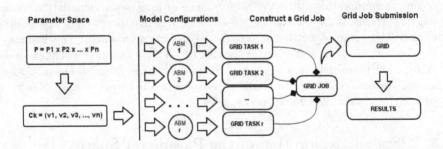

Fig. 1. Parameter space parallel exploration process overview

We propose the construction of grid jobs with r model instances with the same parameter configuration, where r is the number of runs we want to execute for each parameter configuration (as previously described in figure 1). This assures that we are coupling together model instances with the same expected execution time. The ideal number of jobs to be submitted at the same time to the grid depends on the machines available, there is no magic number for it as we can have an infinite number of possible grid configurations. We provide an empirical performance analysis for a small computer grid to make an assessment of the expected performance, the results can however be extrapolated for other grid configurations.

3.2   Formalising the Parallel Exploration Process

We can now formally describe the simple parallelism process that can reduce the time taken in the exploration of social simulation models. One can construct an experiment and distribute its executions over different parameter configurations in the following manner. Consider an experiment $E = (M, P)$ where M is an executable social simulation model and P is the parameter space of the model. The parameter space P is of the form $P = P_1 \times P_2 \times \ldots \times P_n$ where P_k is the range of all possible values we want to consider for parameter k.

A model M behaves like a function $M : C \to M$, with $C \subseteq P$. M behaves like a function taking a set of parameter values which we will call configuration $C = (v_1, v_2, \ldots, v_n)$ where $v_k \in P_k$. The model execution over the configuration changes the state of this model which we can later analyse to extract results.

We define a grid task as a function $T_k : M \times C_k \to R_{T_k}$ where M is a simulation model and C_k is one of the $|P|$ possible configurations of the experiment's parameter space P. R_{T_k} is an entity representing the results produced by the task equivalent to executing the M over C_k.

A job is a work unit in a grid composed of tasks and it is defined as $J_k = \{T_{k1}, T_{k2}, \ldots, T_{kr}\}$. In this case a set of r tasks with the same configuration.

Consider now a grid $G = \{g_s, g_1, g_2, \ldots, g_m\}$ where m is the number of machines in that grid and g_s represents the grid server. We submit a job J_k to a grid server g_s, the grid server automatically decomposes J_k in its elementary r tasks (one task for each run over the parameter configuration C_k) and distributes each task T_k to each available machine $g \in G$ with $g \neq g_s$, balancing the workload between the different machines.

A grid job submission can then be denoted as $J_{\phi k} : J_k \times g_s \to R_k$ where J_k is the job being submitted to the grid, g_s is a grid server that receives the job submission and R_k is the set of results produced by executing the J_k job tasks over the same configuration C_k. In summary a job execution is the computation of r runs over the same parameter configuration. A job execution is done by submitting it to the grid, waiting for the task executions and collecting the results.

An experiment E is then distributed by creating a set of jobs J where $|J| = |P|$, being $|P|$ the number of configurations present in the parameter space P. From the total set of jobs J we create a set of $|J|$ job submissions J_ϕ and execute them to get our social simulation experiment results.

3.3   Performance Gains

The gains in performance one can get from using multiple processing units to execute instructions in parallel depend on the structure of the system. We can however have a general idea of how this process works.

To help us understand the general concept of parallel computation considering multiple processing units, we can refer to *Amdahl's Law* [10]. Simply put, *Amdahl's Law* states that if you enhance a fraction of code f by a speed-up S, the overall speedup (or performance gain in terms of speed) is:

$$Speedup_{enhanced}(f, S) = \frac{1}{(1-f) + \frac{f}{S}} \tag{1}$$

Note that f is the portion of your code that can be executed in parallel and S is the speedup ratio analogous to the number of processing units available to distribute the code execution.

This law has also important corollaries that state that:

- When f is small, optimisations will have little effect.
- As S approaches infinity, speedup is bound by $1/(1-f)$.

When talking about a computer grid, the concept of speedup enhancement is similar but we have to take into account that the processing units are not centralised in the same machine but rather distributed over multiple heterogeneous machines and connected to the grid server by the means of an existing computer network. This configuration introduces communication overheads proportional to the number of machines contained within the grid.

Adding multiple machines would improve the time it takes to deploy a complete social simulation experiment exploration (as we are adding more processing units to the system) but adding more machines not only speeds up the exploration of a social simulation parameter space, but also adds more communication overhead to the system.

The speedup ratio we get from *Amdahl's Law* is an empirical measure of parallel performance. This can be described more generally as:

$$Speedup_{enhanced}(S) = \frac{\Theta_{E1}}{\Theta_{ES}} \tag{2}$$

where Θ_{E1} is the time it takes to run an entire experiment on a single processing unit and Θ_{ES} is the time it takes to run an entire experiment on S processing units. We reduce the time required to execute an entire experiment by running our tasks in parallel, distributing them across the S processing units.

As an example, consider a simple experiment with a parameter space consisting of exactly one configuration C_i (which is executed r times). With one parameter configuration, we perform a job submission $J_{\phi i}$ which submits a job J_i with r tasks. If we consider a task as the most basic unit that can be executed in parallel, we can say that our experiment can be totally executed in parallel. With $S = r$ we can execute every task concurrently. We can define our grid as $G = \{g_s, g_1, g_2, \ldots, g_r\}$ where g_s is the grid server and g_k is a grid node with $1 \le k \le r$. Given a job submission, the job leaves the grid when all de tasks are executed. Moreover, the time it takes to complete a job in the grid is equivalent to the maximum execution time of the tasks within that job [7]. To calculate the speedup from the usage of a grid we then instantiate the terms from equation 2 as:

$$\Theta_{E1} = \sum_{k=1}^{r} \Theta_{T_{ik}}, \forall T_{ik} \in J_i \tag{3}$$

$$\Theta_{ES} = max(\Theta_{T_{ik}}), \forall T_{ik} \in J_i \qquad (4)$$

where Θ_{E1} is the time we need to execute all the r tasks in a single processor, Θ_{ES} is the time it takes to execute all the tasks in the grid with S processing units available and $\Theta_{T_{ik}}$ is the time it takes to execute the task T_{ik} in a single processing unit.

The expression is not yet complete as we have to take into account the network communication overheads (as previously described). The overheads considered are:

- the job submission from the client g_c to the grid server g_s (denoted as $L_{g_c g_s}$);
- the task delivery from the grid server g_s to a grid node g_n ($L_{g_s g_n}$);
- the task result delivery from a grid node g_n to the server g_s ($L_{g_n g_s}$);
- the result delivery from the server g_s to the client g_c ($L_{g_s g_c}$).

We can now rewrite the previous term Θ_{ES} accordingly as:

$$\Theta_{ES} = L_{g_c g_s} + \Delta L + L_{g_s g_c} \qquad (5)$$

with

$$\Delta L = max(L_{g_s g_k} + \Theta_{T_{ik}} + L_{g_k g_s}) \qquad (6)$$

where $\Theta_{T_{ik}}$ is the time it takes to execute the task T_{ik} at the grid node g_k. Note that each task is executed at exactly one grid node.

Substituting the terms in equation 2 we get the speedup enhancement expression for the execution of a single grid job J_i with r tasks and r processing units available:

$$Speedup_{enhanced}(r) = \frac{\sum_{k=1}^{r} \Theta_{T_{ik}}}{L_{g_c g_s} + \Delta L + L_{g_s g_c}}, \forall T_{ik} \in J_i \qquad (7)$$

In summary, the limits for the speedup gains in a given grid are closely related to the maximum time of execution of each model instance (which may not be constant) plus the communication overheads of job submission, task distribution and result collection. To have a better idea on how to analyse the performance of a computer grid the reader should refer to [7].

3.4   Grid Performance Test

To help on the visualisation of the previously discussed grid performance gains, we perform a simple experiment. We consider the submission of a single job to the grid and vary the number of tasks within the job. We measure the job execution time at the client (this time includes the communication overheads) and observe how the number of tasks being executed at the grid affect the grid performance.

The experiment consists in creating "dummy" grid tasks that just wait 1000 milliseconds and then terminate. With all the tasks taking exactly one second to be executed, we submit a single job to the grid assigning an increasing number of tasks to this job. We use this to analyse the behaviour of the grid for a different numbers of tasks to be executed in parallel. Each job submission configuration is repeated for 50 independent runs.

In figure 2 we can see the average job execution time in the grid, versus the time it would take to execute all the job tasks sequentially. The grid used is composed of two 8-core and seven dual-core computers.

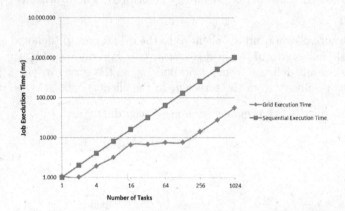

Fig. 2. Average job execution time (in ms) for different numbers of tasks within this job. Each task takes exactly 1000 milliseconds to be executed. We measure the time it takes to execute the job in the grid (in blue) and also display the time it would take to execute all the tasks sequentially (in red).

As we can see in figure 2 and 3, if a job has few tasks, the execution time does not improve much. This is due to the load balance done by the grid server. The grid distributes the tasks in groups to avoid the excess of communication flooding the grid (which is particularly useful if this grid is a shared resource with multiple distinct clients submitting jobs at any given time). What this means is that the grid may choose for example to send a group of four tasks to a machine with only two processing units. As such, some tasks will be executed sequentially in this case. In figure 3 we can see the speedup ratio observed for this grid. The speedup is roughly optimal when we maintain 128 tasks in the grid. This experiment is useful to observe the limitations of the grid. This basically dictates that for the submission of various grid jobs in parallel, with each job containing 50 runs for the same experiment configuration, the performance would not improve if we submit more than two / three jobs at the time (for the grid used in this example).

As we discussed previously, when dealing with the performance gains in a grid, the execution time of a job is bound by the maximum execution time of the tasks within that job. As the user has to perform multiple runs for each parameter configuration, the best approach is to organize the experiment with

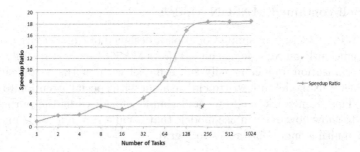

Fig. 3. Speedup ratio observed for different numbers of tasks in a single job submission to a grid with 30 processing units. These processing units correspond to two 8-core and seven dual-core computers.

jobs that correspond to parameter configurations and tasks that represent runs of such configurations. Packing multiple runs for the same configuration in the same job is an elegant solution, as the expected task execution time is similar. Packing different configurations within the same job could cause situations like a group of very fast executing tasks being stalled by a long execution task. This is, tasks representing social simulation models that terminate very fast being stalled by other tasks containing a configuration that causes the enclosed model to take much more time to terminate its execution.

4   Combining MASON with JPPF: A Working Example

In this section we briefly describe the two technologies considered for the parallel execution of simulation runs and explain how to combine them. The working example code provided respects the structural properties presented.

4.1   JPPF Overview

Java Parallel Processing Framework (JPPF) [5], is an open-source, Java-based, framework for parallel computing. Basically it allows us to construct a grid with no effort. A grid is composed by one or more *grid servers* that handle job requests and manage the workload. Connected to those servers are the *grid nodes*. These are computers added to the system in a plug-and-play fashion. Finally, we have the *grid clients* which create and submit jobs to the grid servers. This framework provides facilities that enable us to deployment simple agent-based MASON models to be executed in parallel.

We focus on two basic elements: the first is a self-contained MASON agent-based model (by self-contained we mean that this model has everything that it needs to be executed anywhere on the grid once it is configured properly); the second is the JPPF grid client that allows us to submit a social simulation experiment to the grid.

4.2 Self-contained MASON Models

MASON is a multi-agent simulation toolkit designed to support large numbers of agents efficiently on a single machine [11]. As MASON models are fully separated from visualisation, one can easily run a model without the graphical interface layer. MASON models are written in Java but with special attention to efficiency issues. This framework is elegant and simple enough to fit the purpose of this paper: to show how one can use models that usually run in a single machine and submit multiple model instances to a grid.

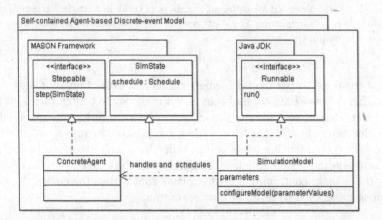

Fig. 4. UML diagram describing the fundamental elements of the MASON framework. These elements are encapsulated in a *Java Runnable* to be submitted as a grid job, allowing the parallel exploration of social simulation parameter spaces.

MASON provides two essential building blocks for any model which is a *Sim-State* class that represents the discrete event simulator itself and a *Steppable interface* which we extend to create our agents (see figure 4). To create a self-contained simulation model we developed a simple *MASON* model by extending the referred building blocks and implement *Runnable* interface from *Java* (making the model suitable for execution in a thread, for instance) putting all the code necessary for the model to be executed in the "run" method. Finally, we want this model to be configurable prior to its deployment to the grid, so we create a method to accomplish that task and receive all the parameters necessary to the model prior to its execution. The basic *U*ML overview over the developed MASON model can be seen in figure 4.

4.3 Creating a Grid Client

To submit multiple jobs as described in the previous section we developed a JPPF grid client experiment runner. The experiment runner performs the following tasks:

1. scan through the parameter space;
2. create multiple MASON model instances with the various parameter values;
3. assign the model instances to grid tasks;
4. construct grid jobs containing those tasks;
5. submit the jobs to the grid;
6. collect the results;

Figure 5 shows the *UML* model for the developed grid client. This diagram depicts the fundamental elements for a JPPF grid client and how these are combined with the self-contained MASON model.

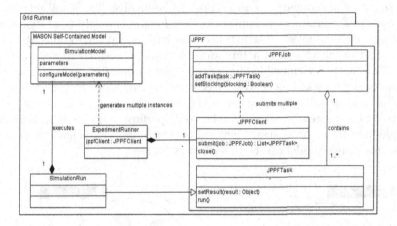

Fig. 5. UML diagram depicting the fundamental elements that allow the creation of grid clients and how one can integrate the self-contained MASON model to submit simulation models as grid jobs

The working example provided contains examples of both sequential (blocking) job submission and parallel (non-blocking) job submission. A blocking grid job submission is one where we submit a job and wait for its completion before submitting the next. A non-blocking submission is one where we may submit multiple jobs to the grid and collect the results asynchronously.

4.4   Context-Switching Model

This section describes the model included in the working example provided with this paper. An agent-based model of social context switching described by [1]. This model deals with the exploration of the influence of different network topologies. This choice resides on the simplicity of the model which makes it suitable to demonstrate the usefulness of using a simple grid system to enhance the speed of parameter space exploration. In this model a society of agents engages in a very abstract game: the consensus game. Each agent has to make a choice towards one

of two possible options which are basically arbitrary. The objective of the game
is to reach a global consensus being the option that gets collectively selected,
irrelevant. What is important is that overall agreement is achieved. The results
we observe from this model are for instance the overall speed of convergence
toward one of the two choices.

In the approach presented in [1], agents have the chance of changing the
option when they have an interaction with another agent in their neighbourhood
(context), by playing the majority game: agents keep track of their previous
interactions and choose the option that they have seen most often in the past.
This game resembles a simple binary voter model and can thus be easily related
to existing literature [8,3].

In most target phenomena, social agents will be involved in several relations
simultaneously. This concept is applied in the model on the study of dynamic
consequences of the topological structures underlying social simulations, so opt-
ing for a "first order approach, actors and relations between them are a given
problem. The agents are embedded in multiple relations represented as static social networks and they switch contexts (see figure 6) with some frequency which
is treated as a probabilistic parameter of the model. In this case the agents are
only active in one context at a time and can only perform encounters with available neighbours from the context they are currently in. The behaviour of the
agents in this simple model can be described as follows:

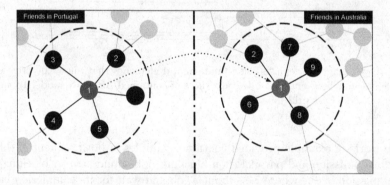

Fig. 6. Example of context switching considering two contexts for social agent denoted
by the number 1. In this case, these contexts are created by two distinct physical spaces.
Common nodes in both neighbourhoods (like agent 2) represent the same social actor
being able to travel between both distinct contexts, representing an acquaintance of
actor 1 in both of them. The dashed circle represents the scope of each context.

1. choose an available neighbour from the current context (neighbourhood of
   the network structure where the agent is currently located);
2. check the current option of the selected partner and increment the memory
   for the number of individuals "seen" with that option;
3. check for the option that has the majority and switch to it if the current
   opinion differs;

4. switch to a random distinct context (located in another network) with a probability ζ_c, which is a parameter of the model related to each social context c.

The described context-switching model was constructed using the MASON framework. For the working example provided, there is both an example to play with the model alone with a simple graphic user interface and an example of a grid client. The MASON model provided uses pre-generated networks, created using the tool B-have Workbench (see [15]).

The provided example code package can serve as a starting point to distribute other social simulation models. In this case we create grid tasks containing context switching model instances and jobs that encompass multiple tasks. We submit the jobs to the grid and collect the results which are the number of encounters necessary to achieve consensus. The parameter space is constructed by combining all the parameters necessary for the model to run.

For example, if we have two social contexts, we need to provide the switching probability for each of those contexts, ζ_{c1} and ζ_{c2}. If we want to span the probability from 0 to 1 with an increment of 0.05, we construct a parameter space $\zeta_{c1} \times \zeta_{c2}$ taking that value range into account. We then submit one job for each parameter configuration, collecting the results upon each job execution.

5   Conclusions

We have shown how one can use *MASON* and *JPPF* to take advantage of parallel computing technology to perform social simulation model parameter exploration. There is no requirement for advanced knowledge on parallel computing to easily implement a grid with the resources available. The approach we describe is perhaps not adequate for models with very complex agent architectures with the need for scalability (agents with complex cognitive architectures for instance). Platforms enabling agents to be distributed by nature (such as JADE [2]) could be more desirable in that case. Nevertheless, our approach has proven advantages when dealing with simple agent-based parameter exploration.

We have described a simple approach to distribute social simulation experiments, executing tasks representing runs over the same model configuration in parallel. This method clusters tasks with similar expected execution times. This minimises the chances of creating jobs that enclose tasks with a high variance in the task execution time. Such a phenomenon would lead to jobs containing very fast tasks being stalled by long execution tasks.

We also provide a working example code package (refer to the section Resources) from which one can understand the basic mechanics of submitting agent-based model instances to a grid and collecting the results. As an example we use a simple social simulation model that measures the number of encounters to achieve global arbitrary consensus in multiple social contexts.

6   Resources

The working example package can be found at: http://labmag.ul.pt/guess/resources/parallel/

References

1. Antunes, L., Nunes, D., Coelho, H., Balsa, J., Urbano, P.: Context switching versus context permeability in multiple social networks. In: Lopes, L.S., Lau, N., Mariano, P., Rocha, L.M. (eds.) EPIA 2009. LNCS, vol. 5816, pp. 547–559. Springer, Heidelberg (2009)
2. Bellifemine, F.L., Caire, G., Greenwood, D.: Developing Multi-Agent Systems with JADE. Wiley (2007)
3. Castelló, X., Eguíluz, V.M., Miguel, M.S., Loureiro-Porto, L., Toivonen, R., Saramäki, J., Kaski, K.: Modelling language competition: bilingualism and complex social networks. In: The Evolution of Language - Proceedings of the 7th International Conference (EVOLANG7), pp. 59–66 (2008)
4. Chen, D., Theodoropoulos, G.K., Turner, S.J., Cai, W., Minson, R., Zhang, Y.: Large scale agent-based simulation on the grid. Future Generation Computer Systems 24, 658–671 (2008)
5. Cohen, L.: Java parallel processing framework (jppf) (2005)
6. Collier, N., North, M.: Parallel agent-based simulation with repast for high performance computing. Simulation (0037549712462620) (November 2012)
7. Iosup, A., Epema, D.H.J., Franke, C., Papaspyrou, A., Schley, L., Song, B., Yahyapour, R.: On grid performance evaluation using synthetic workloads. In: Frachtenberg, E., Schwiegelshohn, U. (eds.) JSSPP 2006. LNCS, vol. 4376, pp. 232–255. Springer, Heidelberg (2007)
8. Groeber, P., Schweitzer, F., Press, K.: How groups can foster consensus: The case of local cultures. Journal of Artificial Societies and Social Simulation 12(2), 4 (2009), http://jasss.soc.surrey.ac.uk/12/2/4.html
9. Gulyás, L., Back, W., Szemes, G., Kurowski, K., Dubitzky, W., Kampis, G.: Templates for distributed agent-based simulations on a quasi-opportunistic grid. In: 20th European Modeling and Simulation Symposium (2008)
10. Hill, M., Marty, M.: Amdahl's law in the multicore era. Computer 41(7), 33–38 (2008)
11. Luke, S., Cioffi-Revilla, C., Panait, L., Sullivan, K., Balan, G.: Mason: A multiagent simulation environment. Simulation 81(7), 517–527 (2005)
12. Mengistu, D., Troger, P.: Performance optimization for multi-agent based simulation in grid environments. In: 8th IEEE International Symposium on Cluster Computing and the Grid, CCGRID 2008, pp. 560–565 (2008)
13. Mengistu, D., Lundberg, L., Davidsson, P.: Performance prediction of multi-agent based simulation applications on the grid. World Academy of Science, Engineering and Technology (2007)
14. Nabrzyski, J., Schopf, J.M., Weglarz, J. (eds.): Grid Resource Management: State of the Art and Future Trends. Kluwer Academic Publishers, Norwell (2004)
15. Nunes, D., Antunes, L.: Introducing the b-have workbench creating reusable components for social simulation experiments. In: Proceedings of the 7th European Social Simulation Association Conference (2011)

16. Stonedahl, F.: Genetic Algorithms for the Exploration of Parameter Spaces in Agent-Based Models. PhD thesis, Northwestern University (2011)
17. Sutter, H., Larus, J.: Software and the concurrency revolution. Queue 3, 54–62 (2005)
18. Terano, T.: Exploring the vast parameter space of multi-agent based simulation. In: Antunes, L., Takadama, K. (eds.) MABS 2006. LNCS (LNAI), vol. 4442, pp. 1–14. Springer, Heidelberg (2007)
19. Walker, L.: Implementing a large scale social simulation using the new zealand best-grid computer network: a case study. In: 18th World IMACS/MODSIM Congress, pp. 1073–1079 (July 2009)
20. Wilensky, U.: Netlogo (1999), http://ccl.northwestern.edu/netlogo/
21. Yamamoto, G., Tai, H., Mizuta, H.: A platform for massive agent-based simulation and its evaluation. In: Jamali, N., Scerri, P., Sugawara, T. (eds.) MMAS 2006, LSMAS 2006, and CCMMS 2007. LNCS (LNAI), vol. 5043, pp. 1–12. Springer, Heidelberg (2008)

A Methodology to Engineer and Validate Dynamic Multi-level Multi-agent Based Simulations

Jean-Baptiste Soyez[1,2], Gildas Morvan[1,3], Daniel Dupont[1,4], and Rochdi Merzouki[1,2]

[1] Univ. Lille Nord de France, 1bis rue Georges Lefèvre 59044 Lille cedex, France
[2] LAGIS UMR CNRS 8146 École Polytechnique de Lille Avenue Langevin 59655 Villeneuve d'Ascq, France
{Jean-Baptiste.Soyez,rochdi.merzouki}@polytech-lille.fr
[3] LGI2A, Univ. Artois Technoparc Futura 62400 Béthune, France
gildas.morvan@univ-artois.fr
[4] HEI, UC Lille, 13 rue de Toul 59046 Lille cedex, France
daniel.DUPONT@hei.fr

Abstract. This article proposes a methodology to model and simulate complex systems, based on IRM4MLS, a generic agent-based meta-model able to deal with multi-level systems. This methodology permits the engineering of dynamic multi-level agent-based models, to represent complex systems over several scales and domains of interest. Its goal is to simulate a phenomenon using dynamically the lightest representation to save computer resources without loss of information. This methodology is based on two mechanisms: (1) the activation or deactivation of agents representing different domain parts of the same phenomenon and (2) the aggregation or disaggregation of agents representing the same phenomenon at different scales.

Keywords: agent-based, simulation, multi-scales, IRM4MLS.

1 Introduction

Today, more and more engineering projects try to cope with complex systems. Complexity can come from the number of represented entities, their structure, or the fact that information is coming from difference sources and is incomplete.

Agent-based modeling is a very powerful and intuitive framework to study such systems. However, the limitations of this approach lead to the development of multi-level agent-based modeling (MAM). It is defined by [13, p. 1] as: "*Integrating heterogenous ABMs, representing complementary points of view, so called levels (of organization, observation, analysis, granularity, ...), of the same system. Integration means, of course, these ABMs interact but also they can share entities such as environments and agents*". From an engineering point of view, MAM reduces the complexity of the problem, so it becomes easier to implement.

F. Giardini and F. Amblard (Eds.): MABS 2012, LNAI 7838, pp. 130–142, 2013.

In complex systems simulations, it is generally necessary to find a compromise between the quality of simulations (amount of information or realism) and their resource consumption (used CPU and memory).

A way to deal with this compromise is to use different models, more or less detailed or treating different aspects of the same phenomenon and that are (dis)activated at run-time, according to the context. This article proposes a methodology to engineer and validate such simulations, based on IRM4MLS, a MAM meta-model proposed by [15,14].

The next section presents recent works in the domain of multi-resolution or multi-level modeling. Section 3 introduces a generic agent-based meta-model IRM4MLS. Then, section 4 shows some possibilities offered by IR4MLS to model complex systems in which different domains interact. Section 5 explains how to construct models with dynamic change of level of detail (LOD), i.e., switching scales or domains of interest. Section 6 gives a tool to measure the quality of multi-level models endowed with dynamic changes of resolution. Finally, we expose the conclusions and perspectives of our work in section 7.

2   Related Works

In this section, multi-modeling approaches, dealing with models at different scales in an engineering context, are presented.

Multi-Resolution modeling [6] is the joint execution of different models of the same phenomenon within the same simulation or across several heterogeneous systems. It can inspire our approach if different models can be considered as different levels. Consistency represents the amount of essential information lost when crossing different models and it is an adapted tool to test the quality of this approach.

The High Level Architecture [19] (HLA) is a general purpose architecture for distributed computer simulation systems. Using HLA, computer simulations can interact (communicate data and synchronize actions) with other computer simulations regardless of the computing platforms. The interaction between simulations is managed by a Run-Time Infrastructure (RTI). [18] developed HLA-Repast, a unified agent-based simulation framework, in which concurrent modules with their own temporality can use global variables through centralized services.

Holonic multi-agent systems (HMAS) can be viewed as a specific case of multi-level multi-agent systems (MAS). The most obvious aspect being the hierarchical organization of levels. However, from a methodological perspective, differences remain. Most of holonic meta-models focus on organizational and methodological aspects while MAM is process-oriented. HMAS meta-models have been proposed in various domains, e.g., ASPECTS [8] or PROSA[22]. Even if MAM and HMAS structures are close, the latter is too constrained for the target application of this work.

[16] present a framework to dynamically change the level of detail in agent-based simulation. That is to say, represent only what is needed during simulation,

to save CPU resources and keep the consistency of the simulation. But this framework is limited because levels form a merged hierarchy, without the possibility of having two levels at the same scale and communication between levels is not explicitly defined.

The possibility for agents to exist in several levels simultaneously is a way to make simulations benefit of a higher power of representation. It permits to 1) simulate nested entities, 2) create agents with concurrent psychological trends and 3) model complex systems implying various domains.

It is possible to model the coexistence of nested entities at different scales. Agents present in different levels can be seen as "gate" between these levels. For example, [17], give the example of cell membrane elements that are the "gates" between the inside and the outside of the cell, i.e., between two scales and exposed to the influences of two different environments.

An agent existing at different levels simultaneously can fulfill a global objective while following its own goals. In [21], authors decompose, with the MASQ model, agents into two bodies: a physical one (individual) and a social one (collective) to do this.

Levels can have different temporal dynamics, independently of other levels. It allows to optimize the execution of complex agents by (dis)activating their bodies at run-time to use the lightest representation [20].

Readers interested in a more comprehensive presentation of MAM should refer to [9,13].

3   IRM4MLS

IRM4MLS is a MAM meta-model proposed by [15,14]. It relies on the influence/reaction model [7] and its extension to temporal systems, IRM4S [10]. An interesting aspect of IRM4MLS is that any valid instance can be simulated by a generic algorithm. The main aspects of this meta-model are presented in this section.

A IRM4MLS model is characterized by a set of levels, L, and relations between levels. Two types of relations are considered: *influence* (agents in a level l are able to produce influences in a level $l' \neq l$) and *perception* (agents in a level l are able to perceive the state of a level $l' \neq l$). These relations are respectively formalized by two digraphs, $\langle L, E_I \rangle$ and $\langle L, E_P \rangle$ where E_I and E_P are sets of edges, i.e., ordered pairs of elements of L. The dynamic set of agents at time t is denoted $A(t)$. $\forall l \in L$, the set of agents in l at t is $A_l(t) \subseteq A(t)$. An agent acts in a level if a subset of its external state belongs the state of this level. An agent can act in multiple levels at the same time. Environment is also a top-class abstraction. It can be viewed as a tropistic agent with no internal state that produces "natural" influences in the level (Fig. 2).

The scheduling of each level is independent: models with different temporalities can be simulated without temporal bias. On an other hand, only the relevant processes are permitted to execute during a time-step. A major application of IRM4MLS is to allow microscopic agents (members) to aggregate and form-up

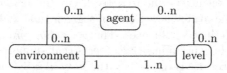

Fig. 1. Central Concepts of IRM4MLS (cardinalities are specifed the UML way)

lower granularity agents (organizations). It can be useful to create multiple levels at the same scale to represent different domain parts of the same phenomenon. In the following, we consider that two levels are at the same scale if they have the same spatial and temporal extents.

4   Multi-level, Single Scale Simulation

In this section we give a framework to improve the integration of agents located in different levels (not necessary at different scales) simultaneously. Then, we show how to take advantage of this concept to simulate complex systems while optimizing the use of computer resources.

4.1   "One Mind, Several Bodies"

In our approach, inspired by [17], agents can be present in several levels at the same time. We propose to decompose agents in a "central" *unsituated* part and a set of n "peripheral" parts, each situated in a given level. Thus, we call *spiritAgent* the unsituated part of the agent which contains its internal state, its decision processes and that cannot act in a level. *BodyAgents* in levels $l \in L$ are the situated part of the agent which contains its external state and the possible actions in its level, like perception of the environment.

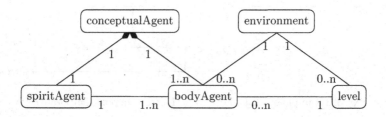

Fig. 2. Class diagram of central Concepts of IRM4MLS with separation of situated-or-not agent parts

ConceptualAgents stand for common agents in classical simulation. **SpiritAgents** only contain the *internal state* of the agent and its *decision module*. **BodyAgents** have to be situated in one and only one level. They contain the *external state* of the agent specific to a level, and an *action module* that indicates: 1) what are the available actions at a given time and 2) what are their results in term of produced influences. The *perception process* must be in this action module. **Levels** contain inactive objects that support agent actions. The only use of **Environments** is to produce the *natural influences* of the level (like the gravity force in a physical level).

To obtain valid simulations with such models, a spiritAgent has to be able to access the external state of its conceptualAgent contained in its bodyAgent when it is active (during the execution of its level). Thus, we can consider the several steps of the life cycle of agents. Each time a bodyAgent is active, 1) it perceives its level (and others perceptible from this one), 2) it sends a part of these perceptions and the possible actions to the spiritAgent, 3) the spiritAgent modifies its internal state and 4) indicates the most appropriate action to be accomplished by the bodyAgent, 5) the bodyAgent accomplishes this action which produces influences in direction of its levels and others possibly influenced by this one.

4.2   Level Temporality

In this section we explain the possibility to attribute a different temporality to each level and how to adapt it to our models. IRM4MLS uses the framework of timed event systems [25]. The scheduling is distributed between levels with no constraint on the scheduling mode (step wise or discrete events). This approach seems more adapted to our problems than the agent one [24] or the system one [11].

Our goal to give to agents the longest possible life cycle which stay coherent with the rest of the simulation. This is done to minimize the computer resources allocated to the agents updating process. [15] propose an algorithm adapted to IRM4MLS which manage the coupling between levels with different temporal dynamics. This is made to apply easily the proposed methods above.

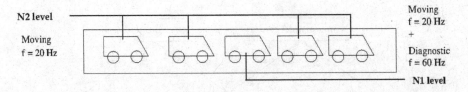

Fig. 3. Example of Multi-Level MAM with different temporalities

The Figure 3 illustrates different constraints which fix the life cycle of agents in a same level. The frequency of a level is expressed in Hertz, indicating how many times a second, it is necessary to execute the updating process of the dynamic state of a level. Let imagine that all functions of an agent possess a minimal frequency beyond which their simulation is not realistic anymore. If a level permits to its agents to dispose of functions with different frequencies, it adopts the higher one, to keep a correct simulation of the functions with this frequency. Therefore, in the example of Fig. 3, the frequency of the level N_1 is equal to $60Hz$ because the diagnostic function of the modeled vehicles needs this minimal frequency.

The other constraint comes from the interactions between levels. If we continue with the previous example, let say that N_2 level needs a minimal frequency equal to $20Hz$, this frequency could be allocated to N_2. However if the N_1 level is influenced by N_2 and has to calculate the reaction induced by these influences at a frequency higher than $20Hz$ (logically less or equal to 60 Hz), it can be necessary to allocate a higher frequency to N_2. Thus, it is necessary to dynamically modify the frequency of a level N and adapt it to the changing needs of the simulation and return it back to its minimal frequency, defined during the implementation phase.

5   Dynamic Change of Level of Detail (LOD)

In this section we give a methodology to apply dynamic changes of LOD in a simulation. First we present the *hierarchical level graph*, which indicates the links between levels and the dis/aggregation functions attached to change the LOD of simulated entities. Finally, we specify when and in which conditions dis/aggregation functions can be applied. In the next part, we give a method to test the quality of the dis/aggregation mechanisms exposed here by measuring the whole consistency of simulations.

5.1   Hierachical Level Graph

Relations between levels are respectively formalized by a digraph, $\langle L, E_H \rangle$ where E_H are sets of edges, i.e., ordered pairs of elements of L. This digraph whose vertices are levels, is called the *hierarchical level graph*. This graph indicates how levels are nested and which couple of levels treats different domain of interest of the same phenomenon.

A *simple edge* represents an *inclusion link* between two levels. For example, an (l_1, l_2) edge signifies that l_2 has higher spatial or temporal extents than l_1. Then the bodyAgents situated in l_1 can be aggregated and the resulting aggregate can be instantiated in l_2. We note that $l_1 \prec l_2$.

A *pair of symmetric edges* means there is a *complementarity link* between two levels. For example, the (l_1, l_3) and (l_3, l_1) edges mean that l_1 and l_3 are at the same scale. Thus a spiritAgent can control several bodyAgents simultaneously present and activated in l_1 and l_3. We note that $l_1 \equiv l_3$.

A *loop* on a vertex indicates levels whose bodyAgents can adopt a similar behaviour. For example, a (l_1, l_1) edge means that the spiritAgent, of some bodyAgents situated in l_1, can be aggregated to form a single spiritAgent which will control these unchanged bodyAgents in l_1. These bodyAgents will have the same behaviour when confronted to similar situations, but will keep their autonomy.

The following rules have to be applied if we want to obtain a coherent model.

Rule 1. *Inclusion and Complementarity links are transitive.*
$l_1 \prec l_2 \wedge l_2 \prec l_3 \rightarrow l_1 \prec l_3$, $l_1 \equiv l_2 \wedge l_2 \equiv l_3 \rightarrow l_1 \equiv l_3$.

Rule 2. *A level cannot be included in itself by a direct or transitive way. This rule is translated by the fact that if we delete all pairs of symmetric edges, there should not be* directed cycles *in the hierarchical level graph.*
$\nexists l_1 \in L \wedge l_1 \prec l_1$

Rule 3. *Two distinct levels cannot share simultaneously an inclusion and a complementarity link, directly or by a transitive way.*
$l_1 \prec l_2 \rightarrow l_1 \not\equiv l_2$, $l_1 \equiv l_2 \rightarrow l_1 \not\prec l_2$.

Each edge which is not part of a symmetric pair of edges is labelled with one or more aggregation function names. An aggregation function name can be placed on several edges.

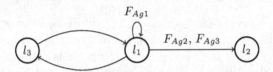

Fig. 4. An example of Hierarchical Level Graph

The (l_1, l_1) edge, labelled F_{Ag1}, indicates that the spiritAgents controlling some bodyAgents present in l_1 can aggregate themselves to form a single spiritAgent controlling all these bodyAgents, through the F_{Ag1} function. The (l_1, l_2) edge, labelled F_{Ag2}, F_{Ag3}, means that the spiritAgents controlling some bodyAgents present in l_1 can aggregate themselves to form a single spriritAgent controlling a single aggregated bodyAgent situated in l_2, through the F_{Ag2} or F_{Ag3} function. These two functions concerns different combination of bodies. And the symmetric pair of edges between l_1 and l_3, with no label, represents the fact that some spiritAgents can control simultaneously bodyAgents situated in these two levels.

5.2   Dis/Aggregation Functions

Content. As shown before, there are two types of aggregation. The first one deals with the aggregation of spiritAgents and the second one with the aggregation of spiritAgents and their associated bodyAgents. The first type of aggregation is used to represent a set of agents with the same internal state, that leads to agents which act similarly in the same situation but which can be place in several situations. The aggregation of several bodyAgents without the aggregation of their spiritAgent is impossible because a body cannot be controlled simultaneously by several concurrent spirits.

Once the hierarchical level graph is fixed, the modeler has to indicate every class of bodyAgent that he decides to place in levels and which class of spiritAgent control these bodyAgents. For each aggregation function the modeler has to precise how many agents have to be merged, the class of aggregated and aggregate agents and how to generate internal and/or external state of the aggregate agent.

In this article we don't give any indication to set the decision module or the action module of aggregate agents or not but we focus on how to aggreagte internal and external states of agents, respectively contained in spiritAgents and bodyAgents. Each aggregation function can be divided into several subfunctions. These subfunctions can be of two types. First type: a subfunction takes the same variable in each agents concerned (spiritAgents or bodyAgents) and aggregates them to obtain a single value to place it in the aggregated agent state. For example, a agent representing a platoon of vehicles has the mean position of all vehicle agents. Second type: a subfunction similar to the first does an aggregation on several variables contained in the agents to aggregated but produces only one value. This can be illustrated by the platoon agent described above. It only possesses one variable in its internal state called "priority" whose value is generated with the compound of the "stamina" and "speed" variables of each vehicle agents in the platoon. Some variables of the agents to be aggregated can be ignored to construct an aggregate.

Notation. An aggregation function consists in creating a composite agent from several agents. Here is the general form of an aggregation function F_{Ag} using for argument n conceptualAgent class, cta (class to aggregate), endowed of an interval, $[min_i, max_i]$, indicating how many instances of these classes are necessary to accomplish this aggregation. For each conceptualAgent class it is precised if the aggregation implies bodyAgents in addition of spiritAgent with the indication of a level l_i where the bodyAgents are situated. The class of the agent produced by the aggregation, AAC (Aggregate Agent Class), is the output of F_{Ag} with its level l if the aggregation concerns bodyAgents. If the aggregation only concerns spiritAgents $l = l_i = \varnothing$.

$$F_{Ag}(\prod_{i \in n} \langle [min_i; max_i] cta_i, l_i \rangle) = (AAC, l) \tag{1}$$

For example, let consider the F_{Ag2} function described in the hierarchical graph below. Let F_{Ag2} aggregates one bodyAgent of class *Leader* and at least 4 to 9 bodyAgents of class *Follower* all situated in l_1 level and their linked spiritAgents to create a bodyAgent of class *Platoon* situated in l_2 level and its linked spiritAgent. Then:

$$F_{Ag2}(\langle [1;1], Leader, l_1 \rangle, \langle [4;9], Follower, l_1 \rangle) = (Platoon, l_2) \tag{2}$$

Aggregation subfunctions have quite the same notation than aggregation functions. It is not necessary to precise the number of concerned agents anymore. But variables, in concerned agents, which will be mixed together have to be known.

For example the subfunction described in the previous subsection can be noted like this:

$$f_{Ag2,1}((Leader.stamina, Leader.speed, l_1),$$
$$(Follower.stamina, Follower.speed, l_1)) \tag{3}$$
$$= (Crowd.priority, l_2)$$

Disaggregation and Memorization Functions. Each aggregation function possesses its disaggregation function and eventually a memorization function. A disaggregation function permits to create several instances of the aggregated agents from the aggregate agent. A memorization function can be used to store some information. Each memorization function is associated to a disaggregation one to generate several agents representing the initial aggregated agents taking into account the last state of the aggregated agents and the system evolution since the aggregation. Here, nb_i indicates the number of agents of each class involved in the aggregation.

$$F_{Disag}(AAC, l, F_{Memorization}(\prod_{i \in n}\langle nb_i, cta_i, l_i\rangle)) = (\prod_{i \in n}\langle nb_i, cta_i, l_i\rangle) \tag{4}$$

These two functions are divided in subfunctions in a similar way than the aggregation function. Let take a platoon endowed of the two position variables, X and Y, representing the position variable x and y of all the vehicles constituting it. The memorization function store positions of all these vehicles. Memorization is not active during the execution of the platoon agent. After the platoon agent have moved in (X', Y') position, it can be disaggregated by recreating the vehicles agents, calculating the value of their x and y variables with X' and Y' and applying the memorized repartition.

5.3   Dis/Aggregation Tests

[16] explains how to decide when agents should be aggregated. He uses an affinity function which measure the similarity of internal and external states of agents. When the similarity is more important than a given threshold he links the two agents. Linked agents with the higher similarity value are aggregated together.

We can use a similar mechanism to decide when to use an aggregation function, but in our case we need one utility function Aff by aggregation function F_{Ag}. If there are several aggregation functions which concern the same spiritAgents or bodyAgents in the same levels, it is necessary to decide when apply one instead of another. There are three possibilities. 1) The choice of F_{Ag} is done after measuring the affinity of agent groups with all Aff and the aggregate are instantiated each time, choosing the group with the higher affinity, until there is no group. 2) It is also possible to impose an order to test different F_{Ag}. All groups with a high affinity for one F_{Ag} are aggregated, then the next F_{Ag} is tested until there is no more F_{Ag}. 3) The choice of F_{Ag} can be done by a mix of the two previous methods. An partial order is defined on $F_{Ag}s$ space. And if there is no precedence link between different F_{Ag}, we apply the first method to aggregate agents considering that the model F_{Ag} only contains these F_{Ag} after that we continue following the established order.

6 Measuring Consistency

[6] uses the notion of consistency to measure the quality of simulations dealing with models of different resolution. "Consistency between a high-resolution model **M** and a low-resolution model **M'** is the comparison between the projected state of an aggregate of high-resolution entities which evolved in **M**, and the projected state of the same aggregate initially controlled by **M'**".

It is more intuitive to base the comparison on the evolution of the more detailed model instead of the aggregate model because it has a higher resolution and possesses more significant information.

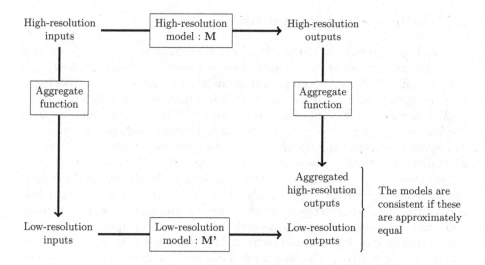

Fig. 5. Weak consistency, according to [6]

Before modeling the system, it is necessary to locate the significant simulation elements. These elements can be in the internal (spiritAgent) or external (bodyAgent) states of agents or in their environment. Once these elements are identified, several simulations are launched with the same parameters (initial state and execution time) using only the most detailed levels, carrying the more information but the most expensive one. At the end of the simulations execution a mean state of the identified elements is recorded. The same process is done with the model using dynamic change of LOD. Then the dissimilarity is measure between these two recording to calculate the consistency.

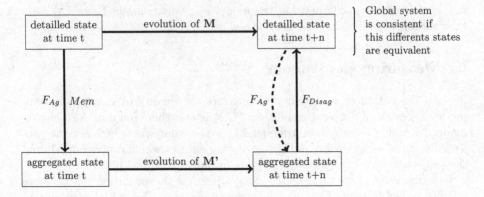

Fig. 6. Strong consistency, according to [6]

7   Conclusion and Perspectives

This article introduces a methodology and theoretical tools to engineer and validate multi-level agent based simulations with dynamic change of LOD.

It is applied in the european project InTrade[1]. This project deals with logistic in european container ports endowed with Autonomous Intelligent Vehicles (AIV). Partners involved in this project work at different scales and use simulation tools adapted to it (SCANeRstudio or Flexsim Container Terminal [2]). The agent-based platform MadKit[3] is used to make models coexist in a single simulation. Results are visualized with SCANeRstudio or Flexsim CT.

An interesting perspective of this work would be to find better ways (cheaper or more realistic) to decide when simulated entities should be (dis)aggregated. It is closely related to the emergence detection and reification problem [5]. Two main approaches have been proposed to tackle this issue: a statistical one (*e.g.*, [1,2,12,23]) and a symbolic one [4,3]. It would be interesting to integrate them.

Another perspective is the integration of organizational concepts, such as *Systems of Systems* (SoS), in our methodology. It would allow to explicitly represent system or group level properties such as goals or missions.

References

1. Caillou, P., Gil-Quijano, J.: Simanalyzer: Automated description of groups dynamics in agent-based simulations. In: Proc. of 11th Int. Conf. on Autonomous Agents and Multiagent Systems, AAMAS 2012 (2012)
2. Caillou, P., Gil-Quijano, J., Zhou, X.: Automated observation of multi-agent based simulations: a statistical analysis approach. To appear in Studia Informatica Universalis (2013)

---

[1] http://www.intrade-nwe.eu/

[2] http://www.intrade-nwe.eu/orwww.flexsim.com/

[3] http://www.madkit.org/

3. Chen, C., Clack, C., Nagl, S.: Identifying multi-level emergent behaviors in agent-directed simulations using complex event type specifications. Simulation 86(1), 41–51 (2010)
4. Chen, C., Nagl, S., Clack, C.: A formalism for multi-level emergent behaviours in designed component-based systems and agent-based simulations. In: Aziz-Alaoui, M., Bertelle, C. (eds.) From System Complexity to Emergent Properties, Understanding Complex Systems, vol. 12, pp. 101–114. Springer (2009)
5. David, D., Courdier, R.: See emergence as a metaknowledge. a way to reify emergent phenomena in multiagent simulations? In: Proceedings of ICAART 2009, Porto, Portugal, pp. 564–569 (2009)
6. Davis, P., Hillestad, R.: Families of model that cross levels of resolution: Issues for design, calibration and management. In: 25th Winter Simulation Conference, WSC 1993 (1993)
7. Ferber, J., Müller, J.P.: Influences and reaction: a model of situated multiagent systems. In: 2nd International Conference on Multi-Agent Systems (ICMAS 1996), pp. 72–79 (1996)
8. Gaud, N., Galland, S., Gechter, F., Hilaire, V., Koukam, A.: Holonic multilevel simulation of complex systems: Application to real-time pedestrians simulation in virtual urban environment. Simulation Modelling Practice and Theory 16, 1659–1676 (2008)
9. Gil-Quijano, J., Louail, T., Hutzler, G.: From biological to urban cells: Lessons from three multilevel agent-based models. In: Desai, N., Liu, A., Winikoff, M. (eds.) PRIMA 2010. LNCS, vol. 7057, pp. 620–635. Springer, Heidelberg (2012)
10. Michel, F.: The irm4s model: the influence/reaction principle for multiagent based simulation. In: AAMAS 2007: Proceedings of the 6th International Joint Conference on Autonomous Agents and Multiagent Systems, pp. 1–3. ACM, New York (2007)
11. Michel, F., Gouaïch, A., Ferber, J.: Weak interaction and strong interaction in agent based simulations. In: MABS 2003. LNCS, vol. 2927, pp. 43–56. Springer, Heidelberg (2003)
12. Moncion, T., Amar, P., Hutzler, G.: Automatic characterization of emergent phenomena in complex systems. Journal of Biological Physics and Chemistry 10, 16–23 (2010)
13. Morvan, G.: Multi-level agent-based modeling - bibliography. CoRR abs/1205.0561 (May 2012)
14. Morvan, G., Jolly, D.: Multi-level agent-based modeling with the Influence Reaction principle. CoRR abs/1204.0634 (April 2012)
15. Morvan, G., Veremme, A., Dupont, D.: IRM4MLS: The influence reaction model for multi-level simulation. In: Bosse, T., Geller, A., Jonker, C.M. (eds.) MABS 2010. LNCS, vol. 6532, pp. 16–27. Springer, Heidelberg (2011)
16. Navarro, L., Flacher, F., Corruble, V.: Dynamic level of detail for large scale agent-based urban simulations. In: Tumer, Y., Sonenberg, S. (eds.) 10th Int. Conf on Autonomous Agents and Multiagent Systems (AAMAS 2011), pp. 701–708 (2011)
17. Picault, S., Mathieu, P.: An interaction-oriented model for multi-scale simulation. In: The 22nd International Joint Conference on Artificial Intelligence, IJCAI 2011 (2011)
18. Scerri, D., Hickmott, S., Drogoul, A., Padgham, L.: An architecture for distributed simulation with agent-based models. In: van der Hoek, Kaminka, Lespérance, Luck, Sen (eds.) Proc. of 9th Int. Conf on Autonomous Agents and Multiagent Systems (AAMAS 2010), Toronto, Canada, May 10-14, pp. 541–548 (2010)

19. Simulation Interoperability Standards Comittee (SISC): IEEE Standard for Modeling and Simulation (M&S) High Level Architecture (HLA) - Framework and Rules. IEEE Computer Society (2000)
20. Soyez, J.B., Morvan, G., Merzouki, R., Dupont, D., Kubiak, P.: Multi-agent multi-level modeling – a methodology to simulate complex systems. In: Proceedings of the 23rd European Modeling & Simulation Symposium (2011)
21. Stratulat, T., Ferber, J., Tranier, J.: Masq: toward an integral approach to interaction. In: Proceedings of the 8th Conference on Autonomous Agents and Multiagent Systems (AAMAS 2009), pp. 813–820 (2009)
22. Van Brussel, H., Wyns, J., Valckenaers, P., Bongaerts, L., Peeters, P.: Reference architecture for holonic manufacturing systems: Prosa. Computers in Industry 37(3), 255–274 (1998)
23. Vo, D.-A., Drogoul, A., Zucker, J.-D., Ho, T.-V.: A modelling language to represent and specify emerging structures in agent-based model. In: Desai, N., Liu, A., Winikoff, M. (eds.) PRIMA 2010. LNCS (LNAI), vol. 7057, pp. 212–227. Springer, Heidelberg (2012)
24. Weyns, D., Holvoet, T.: Model for simultaneous actions in situated multi-agent systems. In: Schillo, M., Klusch, M., Müller, J., Tianfield, H. (eds.) MATES 2003. LNCS (LNAI), vol. 2831, pp. 105–118. Springer, Heidelberg (2003)
25. Zeigler, B., Kim, T., Praehofer, H.: Theory of Modeling and Simulation, 2nd edn. Academic Press (2000).

Towards the Automatic Identification
of Faulty Multi-Agent Based Simulation Runs
Using MASTER

Chris J. Wright, Phil McMinn, and Julio Gallardo

University of Sheffield, Department of Computer Science,
Regent Court, 211 Portobello, S1 4DP, UK

Abstract. Testing a multi-agent based model is a tedious process that involves generating very many simulation runs, for example as a result of a parameter sweep. In practice, each simulation run must be inspected manually to gain complete confidence that the agent-based model has been implemented correctly and is operating according to expectations. We present MASTER, a tool which aims to semi-automatically detect when a simulation run has deviated from "normal" behaviour. A simulation run is flagged as "suspicious" when certain parameters traverse normal bounds determined by the modeller. These bounds are defined in reference to a small series of actual executions of the model deemed to be correct. The operation of MASTER is presented with two case studies, the first with the well-known "flockers" model supplied with the popular MASON agent-based modelling toolkit, and the second a skin tissue model written using another toolkit—FLAME.

1   Introduction

Multi-agent based modelling and simulation is an increasingly popular form of paradigm that is helping scientists, industrialists and policy makers develop their understanding of natural systems, make forecasts, and predict the impact of potential future changes [17], [3], [4], [8]. The need for rigorous model testing and testing tools is becoming ever greater, since model errors can have potentially disastrous consequences, including financial loss [16] and incorrect scientific conclusions [5]. One barrier to the thorough testing of simulation models is the time that must be spent manually inspecting a potentially enormous number of simulation executions for potential errors, which may have been produced as the result of common verification procedures such as parameter sweeps.

This paper presents MASTER (Multi-Agent based Simulation TestER). MASTER is a testing framework that aims to semi-automatically detect "suspicious" simulation runs that may indicate a fault in the implementation of a multi-agent based model. MASTER works by observing a series of simulation runs believed by the modeller to represent the "normal" behaviour of the model. The modeller then specifies a set of assertions that place bounds on which particular simulation properties of the model may deviate from those already observed. In addition, a

F. Giardini and F. Amblard (Eds.): MABS 2012, LNAI 7838, pp. 143–156, 2013.

series of so-called "facts" about the model may also be specified—states of the simulation which should never occur. MASTER then monitors further, potentially extensive, simulation executions of the model—automatically flagging up executions that deviate from normal behaviour or violate some specified fact. The end result is a smaller set of simulation runs, flagged up as suspicious, to be further examined by the modeller.

The MASTER framework was originally written for use with the MASON agent-based modelling toolkit [12], but has since been extended for FLAME [10]. This paper describes the use of MASTER with the simple flockers model supplied with MASON. Results are also presented showing the detection of suspicious runs when the code of the flockers model is randomly mutated to introduce small faults. A further case study is presented with a real-world skin tissue model [17] written for FLAME. White noise is injected into key statistics collated from the model, the presence of which is identified by MASTER.

The contributions of this paper are therefore as follows:

1. A technique for semi-automatically identifying "suspicious" simulation runs of an agent-based model, using past simulation data and modeller annotations
2. An implementation of this technique into a tool, MASTER
3. An investigation into the capabilities of the technique with two case studies, the first with the flockers model and the second with a real-world skin tissue model.

The remainder of this paper is organized as follows. Section 2 describes our technique for identifying suspicious simulation runs for multi-agent based models, implemented into the MASTER tool. Section 3 then presents the usage of MASTER with the well-known flockers model provided with the MASON Java-based agent modelling and simulation toolkit. Section 4 then presents results when MASTER is used with a real-world skin tissue model. Section 5 then presents related work while Section 6 closes with concluding remarks and avenues for future work.

2   The Technique Implemented by MASTER

In normal software testing practice, test cases are evaluated with respect to a specification of a system. However, agents tend to perform actions in a probabilistic or non-deterministic manner, meaning that—given exactly the same circumstances—an agent may choose do something different from one simulation to the next; while the interaction of agents can give rise to complex emergent behaviours, which by their nature are unpredictable and hard to specify precisely. When a specification is not present, a system is evaluated by a software tester who has a detailed knowledge of the system's requirements and which behaviours constitute correct or incorrect behaviour. However, the manual evaluation of long simulation runs is a time-consuming and laborious process.

For a model of any reasonable complexity, generating and evaluating all possible simulation runs is an intractable task. The approach taken by the MASTER framework is to capture data from a small set of simulation runs believed to adequately represent the principal "behaviours" of a model. Following this, a much larger number of simulations can then be run and automatically checked for similarity with those previously observed model executions. A deviation from "normal" behaviour may indicate that the simulation run has exposed a previously undetected fault in the underlying code of the model. The extent of the deviation at which a simulation run is deemed to be "suspicious" is specified by the modeller. Furthermore, the modeller can specify "hard" constraints about a model that are independent of observed model executions—e.g., an agent should never move off the bounds of the grid representing the world in which they inhabit.

The various stages involved in using MASTER are depicted in Figure 1 and can be summarised as follows:

1. *Capturing* is where information regarding "normal" operation of a model in simulation is recorded from a series of sample executions. The modeller must specify what information is to be captured.
2. *Observation Generation* is where so-called "observations" are created by relating data obtained during capturing with modeller-specified assertions that place bounds on that data. These bounds relate the degree to which certain attributes may deviate in future simulation runs from the values already observed for them.
3. *Testing* involves repeated execution of new simulation runs checking for violations of observations and additional modeller-specified facts. Violating simulations are flagged up to the modeller for further investigation.

In much the same way that a tester must write a test class in an xUnit testing framework (such as JUnit [1] for testing Java classes), MASTER requires the tester to extend a common interface to specify the types of information that needs to be captured from normal model behaviour, along with the formulation of "fact" and "observation" assertions. Unlike JUnit, however, MASTER does not require the tester to write specific scenarios in which the assertions will be tested. Instead, each assertion statement is evaluated against a set of simulation runs and evaluated to see if it holds or not. These simulation runs may be generated as a result of a parameter sweep of a model, or from random starting configurations.

MASTER is written in Java for the testing of models written using either MASON [12] or FLAME [10]. The following sections explain each step involved in using MASTER in detail, with the testing of the simple MASON agent class `SpatialAgent` shown in Figure 2. `SpatialAgent` implements MASON's `Steppable` interface, which simply involves implementing the `step` method to move the agent to a new (x, y) co-ordinate at each time step of the simulation.

Capturing. Recording every piece of information about a model's execution over several simulations quickly leads to a situation where an enormous quantity of data must be managed. Simulations consist of several time steps, usually involving many different agents all in different states. The *capturing* stage involves

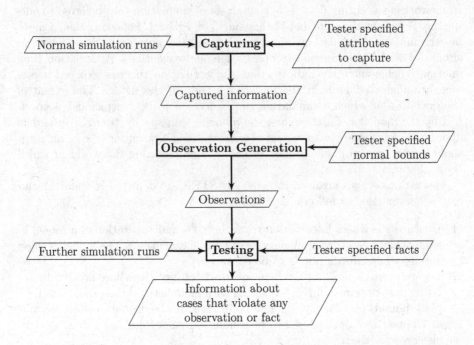

Fig. 1. The process behind MASTER. The "Capturing" stage involves recording specified information over a number of example simulation runs exhibiting "normal" behaviour. The "Observation Generation" stage is the process of combining recorded information and tester-specified bounds of deviation with respect to that information. The final "Testing" stage is where new simulation runs are evaluated against observations and "facts"—additional hard constraints specified by the tester.

```
public class SpatialAgent implements Steppable {
  private int x, y;

  public SpatialAgent(int x, int y) {
    this.x = x; this.y = y;
  }

  public void step(SimState state) {
    x = state.random.nextInt(100);
    y = state.random.nextInt(100);
  }
}
```

Fig. 2. A simple agent for demonstrating testing with MASTER. At each simulation time step, the agent moves to randomly-chosen co-ordinates.

the tester writing code using the MASTER framework to track and capture specific types of data only. This reduces the quantity of data to be stored, managed, and the cost of later analysis. It also allows for richer types of information to be collated other than just raw agent state information. For example, the tester can specify that a computed value such as distance travelled by a particular agent be captured, by tracking the co-ordinates of that agent over different time steps.

In order to track specific data values in simulation using MASTER, the tester must write a *tracker* class that extends MASTER's abstract `Tracker` class. A tracker describes how raw values are captured from the state of a particular agent. An example tracker for a `SpatialAgent` can be seen in Figure 3. It is called "XMinTracker", and captures the minimum x co-ordinate value of the particular agent attached to the tracker at a time step of the simulation. Raw x co-ordinates are obtained using MASTER's `Reflector`, which uses Java's reflection mechanism the access the private instance variables of an agent. Information regarding what is to be accessed is specified using a "locator". A locator is simply an object that describes the sequence of method calls or instance variables required to retrieve some desired information about an agent (or set of agents).

```
public class XMinTracker extends Tracker {
    SpatialAgent agentBeingTracked;
    Locator locator;
    int min;

    public XMinTracker(SpatialAgent spatialAgent) {
        agentBeingTracked = spatialAgent;
        locator = new Locator("x");
    }

    public boolean capture() {
        int x = Reflector.retrieveInt(agentBeingTracked, locator);
        if (x < min)
            min = x;
        return true;
    }

    public Infolet getInfolet(long step) {
        return new XMinInfolet(locator, step, min);
    }
}
```

Fig. 3. Tracker code to capture the minimum x co-ordinate value of a spatial agent over the course of a simulation

Note that the MASTER tracker code is kept entirely separate from the MASON agent code. MASTER does not require special hooks to be inserted into MASON code in order to test it. Trackers must be attached to a simulation so that data can be captured. In attaching a tracker, the tester must specify the number of time step intervals for which the data will be captured using the capture method. That is, an interval of 5 would lead to data being captured from SpatialAgent after every 5th call by MASON to the agent's step method.

Data captured by a tracker is made available after the simulation has finished via Infolet objects. A specific Infolet class is implemented for each tracker to simply return the data captured and the time step that it was captured for (the creation of this class is currently a manual process, but is a step which can be automated in future). MASTER is capable of writing Infolet objects to a text file using the JSON (JavaScript Object Notation) common data interchange format. This is an alternative to binary serialization of objects, and allows for human-readability of information, as well as enabling the captured data to be imported easily into other tools for other types of analysis.

Observation Generation. The second stage in MASTER involves the generation of "observations" for later use in the testing phase. An observation is an assertion relating new simulation data to that already captured in the prior *capturing* phase. The assertion specifies when data from the new simulation should be regarded as "suspicious"; for example if certain values are over some defined boundary, or represent outliers (e.g., are a certain number of standard deviations from an established mean), or are found to be significantly different from those previously obtained—established using some statistical test.

Observations are written as classes that extend MASTER's Observation class. An example can be seen in Figure 4, XLessThanObservation, which asserts that all x co-ordinate values for SpatialAgents are less than the observed minimum value from the simulations examined during capturing—denoted by the variable observedMin. The assertion code is found in the check method, which takes a "target"—in this case a SpatialAgent. The target variable could also refer to an entire MASON SimStep object, so that all agent data from a particular simulation state is accessible. As for Infolet objects, observations may be saved to text files in JSON form.

Testing. The *testing* phase of MASTER involves taking new simulation runs and checking each simulation step against each observation and fact. Observations and facts may be scheduled for checking at intervals rather than at every individual time step. The underlying algorithm for the testing phase can be seen in Figure 5.

If a simulation is found to violate an observation or fact, information is recorded, according to a violation handler, about the simulation and the violation that occurred. This includes the initial configuration of the model, the states of each agent present in the initial time step, any environmental parameters, and the random seed used. This allows the entire simulation to be recreated, and visually inspected if necessary, to allow the tester to understand the nature of the violation and to undertake any debugging steps that may be required. MASTER provides handlers that write violation information to a file or the console, or the tester can provide their own handler that overrides the provided violation handling interface.

```
public class XLessThanObservation extends Observation {
  int observedMin;
  Locator locator;

  public XLessThanObservation(int observedMin) {
    this.observedMin = observedMin;
    this.locator = new Locator("x");
  }

  public Result check(Object target) {
    int x = Reflector.retrieveInt(target, locator);

    if (x < observedMin)
      return Result.newSuccess();
    else
      return Result.newFailure(x);
  }
}
```

Fig. 4. Example code for an observation. The check method is responsible for asserting whether the data from some current simulation (passed into the method as the target object) is violated or not.

```
step ← 1
While (step ≤ maxStep)
      Run the simulation step
      Obtain all observations and facts scheduled for step
      For Each observation or fact
            Check for a violation
            If violation
                  Report all violation details to violation handler
            End If
      End For Each
      step ← step + 1
End While
```

Fig. 5. Algorithm used in the testing phase

3 Case Study 1: Flockers Model

The "Flockers" model in MASON simulates a number of agents exhibiting co-ordinated movement with one another, as seen with natural flocks of birds or shoals of fish. Each flocker agent takes into account local spatial information when deciding which co-ordinates to move to in the next time step; including the direction and momentum of the flockers around it, the need to avoid colliding with other Flockers, coupled with a small degree of random movement. The model also includes optional "dead" flockers, that do not move, but which the live flockers try to avoid colliding with.

In order to evaluate MASTER, an experiment was performed with the Flockers model using Mutation Analysis [9]. Mutation Analysis inserts small syntactic changes to program code, which are designed to mimic typical errors made by programmers—for example, "off by one" errors, where a branching predicate in an if statement is changed from x > y to x >= y. A "mutant" is a piece of program code that has had exactly one syntactic change made to it. The mutant is said to be "killed" when it produces different output from the original program with the same input. The use of Mutation Analysis allows us to artificially inject errors into models, resulting in potentially faulty simulation runs. The effectiveness of MASTER can then be analysed by comparing the number of facts and observations violated by the mutated model simulations.

A special case of mutant is the *equivalent mutant*. An equivalent mutant occurs when a syntactic change cannot result in a change of output [9]. An example of an equivalent mutant is shown below. The mutation changes the relational operator of the inner-nested if statement from "equals" to "greater than or equals". Since i can never be greater than 10 as specified in the condition, there is never any difference in the behaviour of the program, despite the minor change that has been made. In general, detection of equivalent mutants is an undecidable problem.

```if (i <= 10) {```
   ```...```
   ```if (i == 10) {```
     ```...```
   ```}```
```}```
	```if (i <= 10) {```
	   ```...```
	   ```if (i >= 10) {```
	     ```...```
	   ```}```
	```}```

Original program code	**Equivalent mutant**

The original flockers model was sampled 30 times, in which data for the attributes listed in Table 1 were captured for each flocker in the tracking phase. The model was run with 40 flockers (with each flocker set to being a non-moving "dead" flocker with a probability of 0.1), for 1500 time steps. The Flockers model was mutated automatically using the MuJava tool [13], resulting in several hundred mutants, of which forty were selected at random. Each mutated model was then run again to check for observation violations. The attributes listed in Table 1 triggered a violation if they were over two standard deviations from the recorded mean for that property in the previous tracking phase. The purpose of this observation is to trap outlying behaviour of the model.

Each mutated model was run 50 times to obtain an average. The average number of property violations for each mutant can be seen in Figure 6. Each mutant is assigned a unique identification number, with the original non-mutated model assigned an ID of 0 and appearing as the left-most bar in the chart.

The average number of property violations per mutant recorded in Figure 6 correlates well with visual observations comparing original model behaviour with

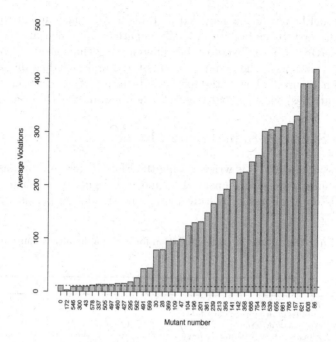

Fig. 6. Average number of observation violations for each mutant of the Flockers model. Violations (outlier values) for the original model appear as bar #0. The dotted line is plotted across the graph to show how the average number of violations for each mutant compares to the original, non-mutated model.

Table 1. Flocker attributes captured during tracking for the flockers model. With the exception of "distance travelled" each attribute is accessed directly from each individual flocker—i.e., from an instance variable or an accessor method of each flocker object.

Property	Description
Position	The X and Y co-ordinates of each flocker.
Momentum	The X and Y momentum values of each flocker. High momentum values encourage a flocker to keep travelling in the same direction.
Avoidance	The X and Y avoidance values of each flocker. High avoidance values encourage a flocker to keep a minimum distance from other flockers.
Cohesion	The X and Y cohesion values of each flocker. High cohesion values encourage a flocker to towards the local area containing the majority of flockers.
Consistency	The X and Y consistency values of each flocker. High consistency values encourage a flocker to move similarly to other nearby flockers.
Orientation	The orientation value (in radians) of each flocker. The orientation value represents the direction the flocker is facing.
No. of neighbours	The number of neighbours throughout the simulation that are close enough to a flocker such that the information regarding those neighbours factor into its cohesion, avoidance and consistency calculations.
Distance travelled	The last position of each flocker is stored in order for the distance travelled by each flocker to be computed and tracked.

mutated model behaviour, as recorded in Table 2. Moving from left to right in Figure 6, the first 16 mutants up to #28—apart from #569—are recorded in Table 2 as having no visually detectable difference in behaviour (i.e., potentially "equivalent" mutants). The first 10 mutants up to and including mutant #427 in the graph Figure 6 show little difference in terms of observation violations (outlying statistics) when compared with the non-mutant #0, the original model.

4   Case Study 2: Skin Tissue Model

The skin tissue model [17] is written using the FLAME multi-agent based modelling and simulation environment [10], and is designed to simulate colonies of skin cells on a laboratory culture plate. The simulation begins with a few

Table 2. Visual descriptions of each simulation for each model after a mutant has been applied

Mutant	Difference
28	*No visual difference detectable*
30	*No visual difference detectable*
43	*No visual difference detectable*
47	Flockers show a strong preference to flying towards the right of the screen
86	Flockers gradually disappear
104	Flockers arrange into up to three evenly-spaced horizontal bands
109	Flockers tend to move in horizontally aligned formations
138	Flockers move to the left only
141	Flockers move vertically only
142	Flockers move vertically only
157	Flockers move downwards only
172	*No visual difference detectable*
196	Flockers attract one another, causing "piles" of flockers to develop
201	Flockers attract one another, causing "piles" of flockers to develop
213	Flockers move downwards only
239	Flockers do not flock
295	Flockers do not flock consistently together as normal
300	*No visual difference detectable*
337	*No visual difference detectable*
356	Flockers stabilise to move consistently along the X axis
358	Flockers stabilise to move consistently along the Y axis
361	Flockers stabilise to move consistently along the Y axis
369	Flockers do not flock, moving as individuals or pairs
427	*No visual difference detectable*
460	*No visual difference detectable*
491	*No visual difference detectable*
497	*No visual difference detectable*
505	*No visual difference detectable*
539	Flockers move downwards only, avoiding each other
546	*No visual difference detectable*
562	Flockers move mostly normally, with occasional erratic turns
569	Flockers move mostly normally, but do not form large groups moving together
578	*No visual difference detectable*
608	Flockers gradually disappear
621	Flockers gradually disappear
655	Flockers move mostly only horizontally to the right only
661	Flockers move mostly only vertically to the bottom of the screen only
666	Flockers move in normal patterns, but slowly and jerkily
754	Flockers move in almost the same direction all of the time
766	Flockers move mostly vertically only

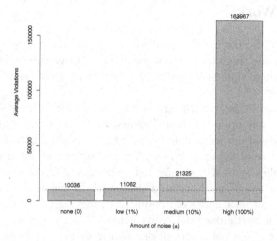

Fig. 7. Average number of observation violations for the skin tissue model for various levels of noise. Violations (outlier values) for the original model appear as noise level 0 ("none"). The dotted line is plotted across the graph to show how the average number of violations for each model with noise compares to the original model without noise.

randomly-seeded individual cells, which form the epicentre of a colony. In each time step of the model, cells progress through the cell cycle and divide, producing new cells. Colonies grow outwards from the initial cell, eventually covering the entire plate. One important aspect of the model is the so-called "differentiation" of a skin cell from one type to another (e.g., to a "corneocyte" skin cell found in the upper-most layers of skin tissue). In the model, cells change type based on the distance from the centre of the skin cell colony of which they are a part. For the purposes of evaluating MASTER, a function was introduced into the model which applied a random proportion of noise to this distance property, thus introducing a source of potential simulation error into the model.

In evaluating MASTER, the model was run for 1000 time steps, with 50 runs performed for tracking and 10 repetitions with three proportional noise levels (low, medium and high). Six skin cells were initially seeded for each simulation run at random locations on the culture plate. In tracking and testing, the distance attribute before a cell makes its first differentiation into another skin cell type is monitored. Figure 7 shows the number of observation violations that occurred when the distance attribute strayed over two standard deviations from the mean found for the property during the tracking step. Low levels of noise (up to 1% of proportional noise applied to the attribute during testing) result in little difference from the original model without noise, but many violations occur with higher levels of noise ($\pm$ 10-100%) and as such are easily detected by MASTER.

5   Related Work

MASTER is a tool for testing the results of whole simulation runs of multi-agent based models. While there has been work on testing agent-based systems, there has been little work that specifically addresses testing of agents designed for simulation.

SUnit, for example, is an existing testing framework for multi-agent systems (MAS), based heavily upon the JUnit framework, that provides an approach for the testing of individual agent behaviour. JAT [6] is similar to SUnit, but uses "mock" agents to send messages to the "agents under test", and then compares the resulting replies against the expected responses. Nguyen et al. [15] propose "eCat", which follows a "goal-oriented" approach in which *means-end* scenarios are described, such that a series of actions (e.g., message passes between agents) should result in a particular goal being achieved, for example a final message containing a given piece of information. Zhang et al. [18] make use of design artefacts, in this case from the *Prometheus* design process, to generate the test data. The data takes the form of "test plans" which describe the various conditions required to evoke a particular behaviour and the predicted outcomes. This, along with a focus on message passing style agents, leads to an "agent-centric" testing approach, where the behaviour of each agent is examined in isolation from other agents and their environment, ensuring that the agent responds correctly to particular messages and percept information.

VOMAS, proposed by Niazi et al. [14], is one tool for validating and verifying multi-agent based simulations. Agents are grouped together by an "overlay" agent. The agents of this overlay are then able to define constraints describing unusual behaviour, and report violations of these if they occur. This validation may relate to both spatial data, i.e. the exact positioning or relative distance of the agents in the simulation under test, and non-spatial data, such as the edges in a graph of connected agents in a social simulation. However, it is not clear how the constrains for the overlay agents are derived, other than from subject matter experts, who provide these during the design of the overlay MAS. Rather than relying on such experts, the MASTER approach attempts to determine the boundaries for these normal values semi-automatically based upon human-approved runs—using some user-specified tolerance outlier formula. MASTER then allows the use of "facts" to allow such expert knowledge to also be incorporated—if there are known domain-specific constraints.

MASTER differentiates itself from the discussed works by both allowing the user to determine the appropriate level of testing, such as applying agent-specific or simulation wide as facts or observations, and reducing reliance on subject area experts, by determining "normal" boundaries from user-approved runs.

6   Conclusions and Future Work

This paper has described a technique for semi-automatically detecting anomalous behaviour in simulations of multi-agent based models. This technique has been implemented into a prototype tool called MASTER. MASTER involves capturing sample data from simulation runs confirmed by a tester to be behaving "normally". Testing of further simulation runs is then directed at comparing whether those simulations have deviated from those witnessed previously automatically. This removes some reliance on expert users, who may otherwise need to manually examine or analyse data produced from a simulation. This allows users to more thoroughly examine the behaviour of their model and ensure, for example, how variation of parameters may affect some emergent behaviour, improving the understanding of the given agent-based simulation.

Future work intends to incorporate of statistical analysis and more sophisticated anomaly detection routines, such as those provided by the libAnomaly [2] library [11], since presently with MASTER, the tester must specify a method for calculating bounds over captured data from "normal" behaviour, which quantifies the ranges to which future behaviour should be compared against. The idea behind anomaly detection systems is similar in principle to that behind MASTER—compare current system behaviour against a representation of normal behaviour. Anomaly detection has been successfully applied to detect malicious JavaScript code on websites, which could harm a user's system [7].

Acknowledgements. This work was funded by the EPSRC grant EP/G009600– "Automated Discovery of Emergent Misbehaviour".

References

1. JUnit, http://www.junit.org (accessed: April 2012)
2. libAnomaly, http://www.cs.ucsb.edu/~seclab/projects/libanomaly/index.html (accessed: April 2012)
3. Bentley, K., Gerhardt, H., Bates, P.: Agent-based simulation of notch-mediated tip cell selection in angiogenic sprout initialisation. Journal of Theoretical Biology 250, 25–36 (2008)
4. Buchanan, M.: Meltdown modelling. Could agent-based computer models prevent another financial crisis? Nature 460(7256), 680–682 (2009)
5. Chang, G., Roth, C.B., Reyes, C.L., Pornillos, O., Chen, Y.-J., Chen, A.P.: Science 314, 1875 (2006); Retraction of: Pornillos, et al.: Science 310(5756), 1950-1953; Reyes, Chang: Science 308(5724), 1028-1031; Chang, Roth: Science 293(5536), 1793–1800
6. Coelho, R., Cirilo, E., Kulesza, U., von Staa, A., Rashid, A., Lucena, C.: JAT: A Test Automation Framework for Multi-Agent Systems. In: 2007 IEEE International Conference on Software Maintenance, pp. 425–434 (October 2007)
7. Cova, M., Kruegel, C., Vigna, G.: Detection and analysis of drive-by-download attacks and malicious javascript code. In: Proceedings of the International World Wide Web Conference (WWW 2010), pp. 281–290. ACM Press (2010)
8. Farmer, J., Foley, D.: The economy needs agent-based modelling. Nature 460(7256), 685–686 (2009)
9. Jia, Y., Harman, M.: An analysis and survey of the development of mutation testing. IEEE Transactions on Software Engineering 37(5), 649–678 (2011)

10. Kiran, M., Richmond, P., Holcombe, M., Chin, L.S., Worth, D., Greenough, C.: FLAME: simulating large populations of agents on parallel hardware architectures. In: Proceedings of the International Conference on Autonomous Agents and Multiagent Systems (AAMAS 2010), pp. 1633–1636. ACM Press (2010)
11. Kruegel, C., Mutz, D., Valeur, F., Vigna, G.: On the detection of anomalous system call arguments. In: Snekkenes, E., Gollmann, D. (eds.) ESORICS 2003. LNCS, vol. 2808, pp. 326–343. Springer, Heidelberg (2003)
12. Luke, S., Cioffi-Revilla, C., Panait, L., Sullivan, K.: Mason: A new multi-agent simulation toolkit. In: Proceedings of the 2004 SwarmFest Workshop (2004)
13. Ma, Y.-S., Offutt, J., Kwon, Y.-R.: MuJava: An automated class mutation system. Journal of Software Testing, Verification and Reliability, 97–133 (2005)
14. Muaz Niazi, A.H., Kolberg, M.: Verification and validation of agent-based simulation using the vomas approach. In: Proceedings of the Third Workshop on Multi-Agent Systems and Simulation 2009, MASS 2009 (2009)
15. Nguyen, C., Perini, A.: Automated continuous testing of multi-agent systems. In: Workshop on Multi-Agent Systems (2007)
16. Simons, K.: Model error—evaluation of various finance models. New England Economic Review, 17–28 (1997)
17. Sun, T., McMinn, P., Coakley, S., Holcombe, M., Smallwood, R., MacNeil, S.: An integrated systems biology approach to understanding the rules of keratinocyte colony formation. Journal of the Royal Society Interface 4, 1077–1092 (2007)
18. Zhang, Z., Thangarajah, J., Padgham, L.: Automated unit testing for agent systems. In: 2nd International Working Conference on Evaluation of Novel Approaches to Software Engineering (ENASE 2007), pp. 10–18. Citeseer (2007)

Author Index